DISAPPEARING DESERT

DISAPPEARING DESERT

THE GROWTH OF PHOENIX AND THE CULTURE OF SPRAWL

JANINE SCHIPPER

UNIVERSITY OF OKLAHOMA PRESS : NORMAN

Portions of the Introduction were published in an earlier version in J. Minkler [Schipper] 2006, "Is Responsible Development Sustainable? The Case of Cave Creek, Arizona," *International Journal of Environmental, Cultural, Economic, and Social Sustainability*, vol. 2 (3), pp. 13–20. Portions of Chapter 2 were published in J. Minkler [Schipper] 2007, "Cultural Productions of Space and Time: Development in the Sonoran Desert," *The International Journal of Interdisciplinary Social Sciences* (on-line), vol. 2 (1).

Library of Congress Cataloging-in-Publication Data

Schipper, Janine, 1970–
    Disappearing desert : the growth of Phoenix and the culture of sprawl / Janine Schipper.
        p.   cm.
    Includes bibliographical references and index.
    ISBN 978-0-8061-3955-5 (hardcover : alk. paper)   1. Cities and towns—Growth—Environmental aspects—Arizona—Phoenix Region.
2. Environmental degradation—Arizona—Phoenix Region.   3. Regional planning—Arizona—Phoenix Region.   4. Quality of life—Arizona—Phoenix Region.   I. Title.
    HT384.U52P46 2008
    307.7609791'73—dc22
                                                                                        2008008454

The paper in this book meets the guidelines for permanence and durability of the Committee on Production Guidelines for Book Longevity of the Council on Library Resources.

1 2 3 4 5 6 7 8 9 10

Thank you Alana . . .
for bringing so much joy, love,
and beauty to this world.

CONTENTS

ILLUSTRATIONS

All photographs are by Sam Minkler.

ACKNOWLEDGMENTS

Support and inspiration for this project came from innumerable sources. Here I wish to acknowledge some of those key sources while keeping in mind that any endeavor springs from the endless creativity and inspiration surrounding us and from many individuals whose presence guides us in ways unknown.

The participants from Cave Creek and the Salt River Pima–Maricopa Indian Community moved me greatly and taught me much regarding life in the Sonoran Desert. I am grateful to have had the opportunity to learn from and work with them. Their voices echo through my mind as I think about our human relationships with nature.

I wish to extend my thanks to Dr. Matthew Bokovoy, acquisitions editor for the University of Oklahoma Press. Matt saw the potential in this project and acted as mentor and guide as we transformed my doctoral dissertation into commentary for a broader audience. Thanks also goes to Alice Stanton, Special Projects Editor, and to Jay Fultz, copyeditor. I also appreciate the many individuals working with the University of Oklahoma Press for their reviews and editing of this manuscript and their many constructive comments. I am especially grateful for the insights and guidance offered by Dr. Theodore S. Jojola, Regents Professor in the Community and Regional Planning program at the Univerity of New Mexico, and by Dr. Dennis Doxtater, professor of architecture at the University of Arizona.

I feel deep gratitude to my good friend and colleague Dr. Karla Hackstaff. Karla read an earlier draft of the manuscript and spent untold hours offering her thoughtful comments and wisdom as I worked and reworked this manuscript. Her humor and her appreciation for my vision encouraged me through the many years that

I have worked on this project. Margot Saltonstall also provided deeply insightful feedback on an early draft and her encouragement and support inspired me to continue the endeavor even through some of its more poignant growing pains. Many thanks to Eliot Schipper for his feedback on selections of early drafts and for his unwavering support of my writing process and vision. Dr. Karen Pugliesi offered critical support during many phases of this project, reading draft chapters and, along with Dr. Warren Lucas and Dr. Kathy Cruz-Uribe, providing institutional support. Special thanks to Debbie Bell for her amazing administrative assistance over the years. Also thanks to Louella Holter, who copyedited several drafts of this manuscript and whose editing gifts have instructed me.

I extend much gratitude to Dr. Bill Burke for so graciously spending his time and effort to help me integrate more creative writing into the final product. Bill's generous and kind nature inspired me greatly during the final stretch of this project. Many thanks to Dr. Sandra Lubarsky for her steady support and belief in the power of the essential messages conveyed in this book. I also thank Sandra for providing the opportunity to share these ideas by inviting me to teach a course on Suburban Sprawl through the Master's in Sustainable Communities program at Northern Arizona University—a brilliant program whose inspired students also helped me to bring key messages across in my writing.

Dusty Hiles has been my good friend, student, research assistant, teaching assistant, and coauthor of an article on the history of planning and development. His many roles in my life have been inspirational, offering innumerable opportunities for learning. Threads of his brilliance weave throughout this manuscript, particularly in discussions on the rational society.

My research assistants have been of the highest quality and have helped to support this project in many subtle as well as direct ways. I wish to acknowledge and thank Becky Springer, Traci Bunker, Amy Fish, Chizuko Yamada, and Matthew Haake.

Many friends and students read drafts and also offered invaluable feedback. Thanks go to Glenn and Karen Williamson and Jim Olsen for their wonderful conversations and years of encouragement and support. Much thanks to Toby Litvin, Todd Sherman, Annette McGivney, Robert DiCarlo, and Alex Voyels for additional comments that helped in ways that they may not have realized.

Thanks go to my parents, Larry and Barbara Berkowitz, for reading very early drafts and offering their honest feedback. Their feedback helped guide the writing of future drafts for a broader public audience. I also want to thank my parents and grandparents for their always loving and continual support of anything I set out to do.

Opportunities at three key institutions of higher learning have played enormous roles in the development of my thoughts about issues of land and development. My time in these places has offered me the skills and resources to make this project possible. I am grateful to have had the chance to learn from many brilliant, generous, and inspired thinkers at Brandeis University, Boston College, and Northern Arizona University.

Finally, this book would not be possible without the patient support of Sam Minkler. Sam helped as a guide and support from its inception. Sam recognized and brought to my attention the possibilities of working with the Cave Creek and Salt River communities. He also brought Spur Cross Ranch to my attention, helped me gain access to the Salt River Community, and spent countless hours driving around the Phoenix metropolitan area photo-documenting the study from its beginning and for years to come. Sam always kept me attuned to the essence of this project so that I never lost my way—reminding me that the land has a language of its own . . . if we would only listen.

DISAPPEARING DESERT

INTRODUCTION

CULTURAL PERCEPTIONS AND SUBURBAN SPRAWL

Under the desert sun, in the dogmatic clarity, the fables of theology and the myths of classical philosophy dissolve like mist. The air is clean, the rock cuts cruelly into flesh; shatter the rock and the odor of flint rises to your nostrils, bitter and sharp. Whirlwinds dance across the salt flats, a pillar of dust by day; the thornbush breaks into flame at night. What does it mean? It means nothing. It is as it is and has no need for meaning. The desert lies beneath and soars beyond any possible human qualification. Therefore, sublime.

—EDWARD ABBEY, 1988

In 1996 Cave Creek, Arizona, was a sleepy little town snuggled into the Sonoran Desert foothills. Unassuming homes in Cave Creek seemed to merge with sun-baked rock. Residents generally avoided "scraping" the land and left the natural flora intact whenever possible. They refrained from introducing nonnative bushes and trees like palms onto their property. Also, they supported zoning ordinances for low-density development, believing that the more spread-out their homes, the less damage done to the land. As a small rural town for the past fifty years, Cave Creek appeared as a slight dimple on the face of the vast Sonoran Desert.

In contrast to Cave Creek rose downtown Phoenix, a mass of glass skyscrapers reflecting the big desert sky and glistening in

3

the shadows of the rugged mountains that surround "The Valley of the Sun." Located fifteen miles south of Cave Creek, Phoenix typifies the modern American city. The Greater Phoenix Chamber of Commerce (2005) describes Phoenix as "a sprawling metropolitan desert area that extends from trendy Scottsdale in the northeast, to Glendale and numerous expanding towns in the west." This modern metropolis has reinvented the meaning of "desert," converting uninhabitable wasteland to land of great prosperity and endless possibility. "Phoenix is a city on a roll" Mayor Skip Rimsza pronounced in his 2001 State of the City address. "Believe me, if you're the mayor, having a city that's on a roll is as good as it gets."

In 1996, Phoenix was indeed rolling along, transforming desert into housing developments at the rate of one acre every hour, or approximately ten square miles of Sonoran Desert every year. In a typical Phoenix development, each home, designed the same as every other home, has a small, well-manicured front lawn with some flowers and a cactus or two. Sometimes rocks, carefully arranged to resemble the desert, replace grass lawns. Miles of red tile roofing extend above the adobe walls that enclose planned communities. American flags fly high, indicating the model home in each development.

In the 1990s, development progressed steadily in all directions because land farther away from the city limits was cheap and available. And one day, in line with patterns of suburban growth found all around Phoenix, a developer proposed to build a master-planned community north of Cave Creek on 2,154 acres called Spur Cross Ranch. Success was guaranteed with a 100-room resort hotel, 656 homes, and an 18-hole golf course sitting amidst some of the most magnificent desert remaining close to Phoenix.

My visits to Spur Cross Ranch revealed a place of incomprehensible beauty. The desert is alive, vibrant with colors that, depending on the time of year, range from the muted yellows and greens of sycamore and mesquite trees to the deep reds,

pinks, and purples of flowering cacti. Barbs of all shapes and sizes seem poised to strike any who dare pass through. They guard succulent plants—plants perfectly designed to endure endless arid days. Some, like the great saguaro, stand defiantly in the same place for hundreds of years, their immense arms reaching out to the sky.

From jagged rocks evolve a spectacular assortment of plants, all of which support each other. Even the wind works with the land, shifting rocks slowly down toward the sea. A lizard does a few pushups in the shade. A butterfly glides by. Cave Creek twists around craggy brush and tumbles off jagged Elephant Butte. The desert humbles me, for there is no way to paint an accurate portrait and the images continually shift from moment to moment, depending on the observer. Edward Abbey came close to capturing some essence of the desert in his haunting accounts, yet even Abbey could not describe the magnificence and so acknowledged: "The desert lies beneath and soars beyond any possible human qualification. Therefore, sublime."

The proposed community in Spur Cross Ranch created quite a stir. Environmental activists accused the owners and developer of lining their own pockets at the expense of primeval saguaro forests, riparian areas,[1] and endangered species. Developers and property rights advocates accused environmentalists of acting like tyrants, limiting freedom, and placing "little bunnies above human beings," as one Cave Creek developer said. Environmentalists nevertheless relentlessly opposed development and soon the effort to preserve Spur Cross Ranch gained national attention. However, it seemed unlikely that this small community (population 3,785), with its even smaller activist network, called "Friends of Spur Cross," could pose a real challenge to the great forces of development sweeping across the Southwest and particularly Phoenix. Every census since the 1940s has recorded increases in Sunbelt populations (Hertz et al. 1990).[2] In the 1990s the South and the Southwest experienced the largest population increases, with the Phoenix metropolitan area ranking as the fifth fastest growing city and fourteenth largest metropolitan area (population 2.6 million) in the United States (U.S. Census Bureau 2000: Tables 2-4). By 2006, Phoenix had added more new residents than any other city in the United States, increasing by 44,456, or 3.1 percent (Christie 2006), with a total population of 1.5 million (U.S. Census, 2006).

The movement to preserve Spur Cross Ranch faced all of the typical obstacles in challenging the developers, who, as one leader of Friends of Spur Cross put it, "have more juice than God." Strong political alliances coupled with huge budgets provide certain advantages to developers that remain unmatched by grassroots organizations. Nevertheless, collective and sustained community action effectively stopped the powerful forces that were driving the development. In November 2000, 77.4 percent of Cave Creek voters backed the first property tax in the town's history, costing the average homeowner about $132 per year for twenty years to preserve Spur Cross Ranch.

In 1996, when just a scattering of homes speckled the Cave Creek foothills, I tried to learn how this modest town managed to challenge and ultimately stop development. However, by 2000 I was noticing something different: the Sonoran Desert foothills were now being developed. By 2001, the foothills were filled with homes and today the untamed desert that once characterized Cave Creek is but a shadow of its former self, existing largely in plots of "un-scraped" land in neighbors' yards.

In the late nineties, Cave Creek stood as a model of a small community that had fought big-money development and won. The ungroomed desert of Cave Creek contrasted sharply with the concrete order that characterizes Phoenix. Today, although Cave Creek continues to develop differently from the surrounding area, only a trace of the desert remains. Why has much of the desert in and around Cave Creek disappeared? Why, despite public policy efforts focused on land growth reform[3] and despite well-organized grassroots efforts promoting land trusts to purchase and preserve land, is this land rapidly transforming?

The rapid changes to the Sonoran Desert foothills are but one example of the type of development, popularly known as "suburban sprawl," that we see shaping millions of acres of forest, cropland, and open space across this country. Suburban sprawl is the pattern of ever-increasing low-density development into undeveloped land and the consequent expansion of metropolitan areas.

Suburban sprawl is characterized by cookie-cutter subdivisions, strip malls, pollution, damage to rural and natural areas, and a legion of highways often jammed with traffic. Architect Vernon Swaback graphically defined sprawl as "the uglification of communities by way of haphazard, hopscotch, unplanned, strip, ribbon, or leapfrog development in low-density, single-use patterns, spread in a monolithic fashion without relief of open space" (1997:37).

The federal government reports that between 1992 and 2002 land was developed at a rate of 2 million acres per year (National Resources Inventory 2002); this translates to the development of 228 acres per hour. Of this, 1.2 million acres is farmland that is lost to sprawling development each year, affecting crucial environmental safeguards like water-quality protection, aquifer recharge, floodwater detention, and riparian and upland habitat (Stuart 2003). The hidden price of sprawl entails fiscal pressures on towns and cities to build the necessary infrastructure to service these outlying areas, diverting business money away from inner city areas, and threats to the ecological integrity[4] of large expanses of land.

Proponents of sprawl point out that urbanized areas account for only 5 percent of the United States' land base. Their arguments against Smart Growth legislation and other initiatives to curb sprawl maintain that such efforts are ideological, draconian, threatening to American property rights values, or, in the words of a Phoenix developer, the product of "zealous environmentalists out to impose their views on the rest of the world." Yet Americans cite suburban sprawl as one of their top concerns (Pew Center 2000). "Sprawl is now a bread-and-butter community issue, like crime," says Jan Schaffer, executive director of the Pew Center for Civic Journalism.

While supporting concerns about the rapid pace of suburban development, I am critical of many efforts to curb sprawl, observing an irony that I have come to call "responsible sprawl." Through "responsible development," "sustainable development," "green development," and so forth, rural land bases get developed, albeit responsibly. This is what happened in Cave Creek, Arizona. Despite intentions to curb sprawl through responsible development, little desert remains. And whether responsible or irresponsible, the urbanization of land has dramatic ecological consequences that often go unacknowledged. A brief review of some of the ecological problems precipitated by development in the desert illustrates why it is vital that we critically examine our building practices there.

URBANIZATION IN THE DESERT

Cave Creek is situated near the northern edge of the Sonoran Desert, which stretches from the southern half of Arizona, runs throughout most of Sonora, Mexico, and slopes south into the Baja Peninsula. Covering about 120,000 square miles, the Sonoran Desert is rich with wildlife living in delicate balance with one another. It serves as home to fifty mammalian species, including coyotes, javelinas, mountain lions, deer, and bats. The gila monster, rattlesnake, scorpion, centipede, black widow, and tarantula also gravitate here. More than eighty-five species of birds live in the northern region, including such southwestern notables as the roadrunner, quail, cactus wren, owl, red-tailed hawk, vulture, and blue heron (Foothills Community Foundation 1990). The desert floor is covered with saguaro cactus, prickly pear cactus, cholla cactus, barrel cactus, ocotillo, palo verde trees, mesquite trees, sycamore trees, and ironwood trees. As urbanization of the desert spreads, many unique species of plants and animals face the threat of extinction.[5] The Sonoran Desert is of particular concern in this regard because it houses one of the most diverse arrays of desert plants and animal species on the planet (Lincoln Institute 2003).

The case of the saguaro cactus—a symbol of the American West—exemplifies the delicate balance maintained by the desert ecosystem. The saguaro depends on and supports a wide variety of plants and animals. As development increases, saguaro numbers dwindle. Efforts to save the saguaro through transplanting do not take into account how that affects its mutually dependent relationship with other animals and plants, all of which are threatened by continued development.

Deserts also play a crucial role in the world's weather systems, acting like giant radiators. About a third of the earth's landmass is arid. Deserts characteristically receive less than ten inches of rainfall per year, have sparse cloud coverage, and are largely located within tropical zones, close to the equator, where they receive nearly direct sunlight. These conditions produce land that absorbs energy during the day. Then, without an insulating cloud cover, the desert surface cools rapidly at night (Goodall et al. 1979:347). Thus, deserts absorb and release radiation, serving to help regulate the temperature of the planet. Furthermore, deserts are among the most fragile ecosystems on the planet precisely because they experience extremes of heat and aridity. Changes to the desert are usually permanent; for example, horse carriage tracks from more than one hundred years ago remain intact on the Sonoran Desert floor. Off-road vehicles have been especially destructive, uprooting sparse vegetation and digging deep ruts that may permanently mar the desert while causing heavy erosion. Destruction of arid land ultimately poses a severe global threat. At the 1992 United Nations Conference on Environment and Development in Rio de Janeiro "desertification" was defined as "degradation in arid, semi-arid and dry sub-humid areas resulting from various factors, including climatic variations and human activities" (1992:46). Desertification affects 70 percent of all dry lands, thus affecting approximately a quarter of the total landmass of the world. Desertification reduces the ability of the land to support life and threatens the abundance and uniqueness of plant and animal life in the desert. Degradation of the desert may erode, salinize, or impoverish soil, and limited water supplies are threatened by overuse and pollution. One can only imagine the vast ecological repercussions of building highways, homes, businesses, and golf courses on this tenuous desert land.

RESEARCHING SUBURBIA

Having grown up in a suburb of Manhattan, I am familiar with the rhythms and structures of suburban life. It wasn't until adulthood, when I flew over the Sonoran Desert for the first time, that I began to understand something that I had always taken for granted: suburbia has not always existed. Growing up in New York and then living in Boston for eight years provided a one-dimensional understanding of land and development. That is, all land was developed. The land rolls in and around the small towns and large cities of the Northeast coast. Vast tracts of undeveloped land, if they exist, are hidden from everyday life. In contrast, the Southwest appears as an empty canvas interrupted by the latticed patterns of suburbia in the making. As Arizona became my home, I witnessed the rapid pace of suburban development. Undeveloped land filled up with tract homes and master-planned communities within months. Within a year, homes covered hills that once appeared as islands covered in saguaro cacti. This hasty development was truly remarkable to me. I felt as though I was experiencing a film on fast-forward—what was undeveloped was, in the next moment, transformed.

I was first inspired to visit Phoenix and the surrounding areas after doing research on development in the Sonoran Desert. Reading about the desert while sitting in coffeehouses, libraries, and my small apartment in Boston was a disorienting experience. Nature and land looked one way from my Boston view and yet my reading materials offered me another view. In particular, I wondered how those living through dramatic changes in the desert experienced those changes. Since I had only lived in urbanized areas, I wondered what it was like for those living in once rural areas to experience dramatic shifts in land use and development. As a sociologist, I designed a study to examine perceptions of the land and development (see Appendix A), and I moved to Arizona. I interviewed members of the Cave Creek community and Salt River Pima–Maricopa Indian Community because those communities stood as clear examples of once rural regions experiencing rapid development. I also spent time in dozens of master-planned communities throughout the Phoenix metropolitan area.

While I attempt to articulate a range of community members' ideas about sprawl, land, and development, I also take the position of an outsider who has something to say about these attitudes—specifically in reference to ecological sustainability. Like sociologist Herbert Gans (1967), I seek to uncover meaning held by community members and also assess the legacy of that meaning in reference to a particular societal value—in this

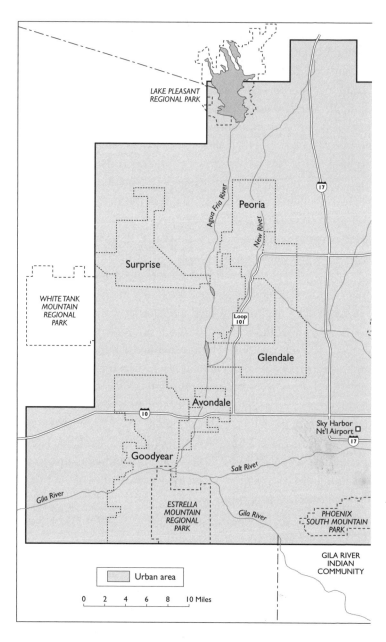

Map of the Phoenix Metropolitan Area. Cave Creek, Arizona, is located fifteen
is located fifteen miles northeast of Phoenix. Fountain Hills, Scottsdale,

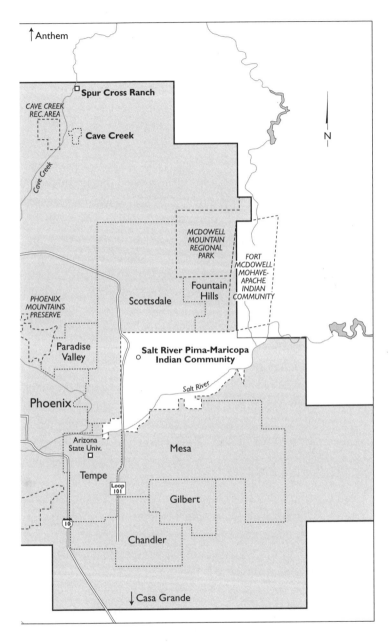

miles north of Phoenix. The Salt River Pima–Maricopa Indian Community
Tempe, and Mesa border the Salt River Community.

case a value of ecological sustainability as widely articulated by community members. Gans assessed whether the post–World War II planned community of Levittown, New Jersey, met certain standards of democracy. I wonder if the meanings that communities create around land and development fit in with their ideas about sustainability and how to care for the land. In broader terms I ask: What is the ecological legacy of sprawl? Critical writing on sprawl has itself faced significant critiques. For example, Lewis Mumford (1961) warned that architectural uniformity would lead to social uniformity. However, Gans felt it was important to accept communities on their own terms and assumed that "people have some right to be what they are" (1967:vi). Mike Davis has reignited scholarship that is highly critical of the social, environmental, economic, and cultural consequences of our sprawling suburbs. In *City of Quartz* (1992), Davis took a markedly acerbic tone when describing the malaise of sprawl's developers who display "malice towards landscape" (1990:6) and offered a counterpoint to utopian views of Los Angeles as a futuristic city.

Other scholars have recently pointed out that focus on suburbia's failures overlooks the "affirmative value of suburbs for those who live in them" (O'Mara 2005) and overlooks the demographic changes that have made the suburbs home to urban migrants, many of whom are from minority and working-class backgrounds (Kruse and Sugrue 2006, Nicolaides 2002, Sides 2004).

Keeping the rich history of analysis of the suburban condition in mind, *Disappearing Desert* aims to give voice to community members who have experienced the pressures of sprawl while also questioning some fundamental assumptions that may serve to promote or control sprawl. Prompted by Donna Haraway's (1991) writing on "situated knowledge," I offer an account of various individual points of view while contributing my own "partial perspective" and remaining aware of how my own position shapes what can and cannot be seen. I use illustrations to ground abstract patterns and theory in everyday life. These examples, taken from community members' narratives, expound upon key ideas and are not intended to serve as an exhaustive account of the full experiences of groups of people and their places. (See Minkler [Schipper] 2000 for fieldwork descriptions). While aiming to convey general patterns of thoughts and draw out specific community members' voices, it is important to note that this book contains only a partial account of community members' experiences.

I have taken a more literary approach to describing findings, keeping in mind the always-incomplete nature of interpreting and conveying others' perspectives. Anthropologist James Clifford (1992) maintains that due to its organic, changing nature, culture cannot be fully understood by the "native" of a particular culture, let alone a visitor. In addition, the visitor can never learn all of the "diverging, contesting, dialoguing, set of discourses in language" (1992:98). Furthermore, human practice cannot adequately be translated into language. Social theorist John Fiske (1992) has pointed out that the expression of cultural practices must be communicated through words, but in the process of reducing practices to language we change their meaning. Anthropologist Clifford Geertz (1973) also observes that, through their writing, social scientists fix cultural experiences, thus rendering those experiences as different from what they "really" are. Ultimately, the writing process changes the very meaning of what has been said and observed. Language fixes meaning, although meaning itself is fluid; something said one way at one moment takes on different meaning or is experienced differently in another moment.

In an effort to avoid fixing experiences and perceptions that are ever-changing, I am more inclined to raise questions and convey a feeling more than a hard reality. In these ways, I take a "humanist" approach, seeking to offer suggestive insights as a sociologist who has examined patterns of ideas in the various communities while raising critical questions intended to inspire further inquiry and augment conversations on sprawl. I specifically hope to engage readers in an inquiry into the part our beliefs play in shaping our sprawling communities and to examine how even our most subtle ways of thinking about land and nature play crucial and often overlooked roles in shaping our built environment. I hope that in the process of reading this book ideas get challenged, questions arise, and new ways of thinking about how we perceive and live on these lands emerge.

THE CULTURAL FORCES OF SUBURBAN SPRAWL

Structural, environmental, aesthetic, and cultural ways of relating to land all shape our built environment. Structural factors refer to the systems and institutions shaping it. For instance, local governmental policies guide where and how land can be developed. Local zoning boards regulate housing density and the kinds of activities that can take place in particular areas—whether particular lots are designated for residential, commercial, agricultural, open space, or industrial use. The highway system is another structural factor that influences our built environment. Previously inaccessible land becomes available for development when new roads are built.

Environmental factors necessarily play some role in how we design our buildings and communities. Differing environmental conditions influence choice of building materials, building designs, and varying approaches to soil erosion. Obviously, those who live in a desert environment with limited water supplies cannot live like those in the rainforest.

Aesthetic desires also influence building patterns. Rachel and Stephen Kaplan question why, in a utilitarian market-oriented society, people value nature in ways that do not generate income. Caring for plants, spending large sums of money on natural settings and landscaping, and widespread decorating of homes with flowers "provide at least circumstantial evidence that nature is important in itself" (1989:1). Indeed, the selling of wilderness depends on its beauty, as evidenced by advertisements selling homes in the desert (see Chapter 3). Developing green building structures may satisfy not only an ethical obligation to tread more softly on this planet but may also serve psychological and aesthetic needs to see and experience nature.

Although structural, environmental, and aesthetic influences permeate our experience of the built environment, this book specifically focuses on those widely held collective perceptions that shape our behavior and choices. I refer to the belief systems that drive development as the cultural forces of suburban sprawl. The dynamic forces underlying any social phenomenon are complex and defy complete understanding or explanation. However, by looking at some aspects of culture we can explore the nature of our attitudes and perceptions and thus begin to identify some of the underlying factors that influence our choices.

Geertz (1973) once defined culture as the collection of stories we tell ourselves about ourselves. Through examining some of our most fundamental taken-for-granted beliefs, we can see how our perception of land and the way that we develop land tell us a story about ourselves and that which we value. This approach— looking at particular social phenomena as a "cultural text" (Geertz 1973) that reveals underlying meaning—raises certain questions when applied to suburban sprawl: What does sprawl communicate to us about what we value? Are those values in sync with or at odds with other values? If we are not happy with the sprawl story, how do we go about rewriting the story? Should we address sprawl by changing the way that we live—for example, by instituting stricter building and zoning codes or legislating growth boundaries? Or should we address sprawl by challenging our own belief systems—that is, by raising our "environmental consciousness"? Both of these orientations— changing structures and challenging beliefs—inspire social change. However, most of the scholarship on suburban sprawl focuses on structural arrangements that produce sprawl and hence focuses on political, legislative, and economic solutions.

This book is not about the structural arrangements that produce sprawl.[6] It is not about our dependence on the automobile as our main form of transportation or the economics of property values, structures of public funding, lack of regional legislative bodies, subsidies to sprawl, or anti-tax ideologies, all of which contribute to our sprawling American communities. Nor is this book about environmental and aesthetic factors that also influence where and how we live. This book is about the cultural forces—those deeply embedded and widespread belief systems that subtly shape our experiences—that drive suburban sprawl.

Each chapter highlights a key cultural force that shapes our conceptions of nature[7] and reflects ourselves as alienated from nature while advancing sprawl. The five cultural forces of suburban sprawl examined here concern the rational society, cultural productions of space and time, the selling of the American Dream, consuming the Dream, and rights wars. Many other cultural forces play important roles in shaping the way we perceive and live with the land. Such factors as patriarchy, religion, and modern technologies also affect the way we relate to land and construct our built environment, but these did not emerge as strong factors in my observations of specific communities. While the cultural forces of sprawl discussed here apply to American culture broadly, they derive from patterns that emerged from particular locations and must be considered in that light.

The five cultural forces examined in this book, aside from shaping sprawl, also shape other aspects of American society. Social scientists have applied these same cultural factors to a range of social phenomena in order to assess how certain assumptions and belief systems influence our social conditions. For example, researchers have looked at how cultural perceptions of space influence technology (Romanyshyn 1989), gender and the workplace (Odih 2003), and social interaction and power (Derber 2000). The advantage of such cultural studies is that they offer novel ways of understanding social problems. They help us see these problems from an outsider's perspective, providing distance so that we can approach the particular issue or problem from a fresh perspective.

I suggest that, when left unexamined, our assumptions about land, nature, and reality help fuel the growth society. Without taking a measured and serious look at our very ways of thinking, we are bound to continue to reproduce the same patterns that originally caused the problems. Hence, I maintain that to end sprawl we need more than political, legislative, and economic policies; we need entirely new ways of thinking and relating to the land.

Dolores Hayden (2004), professor of architecture, maintains that curbing sprawl requires citizen involvement in community decision-making processes. Hayden holds that since research on sprawl consists largely of statistics and technical jargon, we must build a new vocabulary of sprawl that helps us understand and question destructive building patterns. Drawing on Hayden's classifications, this book focuses on *boombergs*, cities with more than 100,000 residents that grow by the tens of thousands with every census. This is the pattern in various cities throughout the United States. The Phoenix metropolitan area serves as a case study; it is an *edgeless city* growing along an interstate highway, and it is experiencing an explosion in residential communities. Within the Phoenix metropolitan area are two communities—Cave Creek and the Salt River Pima–Maricopa Indian Community—that exemplify *rurban development*, that is, urban-scale development in rural areas. Finally, I look at *edge cities*, physically large areas with many office parks and large-scale retail centers bordering the big city, what Joel Garreau calls a "psychological location—a state of mind—even more than a physical place" (1988:xiv).

Disappearing Desert combines social research, social theory, and personal reflection and discovery. The social research focuses on case studies in the Phoenix metropolitan area as well as analysis of advertising from southwestern cities and master-planned communities. Social theory offers historical and cultural contexts for understanding certain aspects of the sprawl phenomena. Finally, through narrative I trace my own growth in understanding the forces of sprawl, the myths that have guided our growth into the desert, and the development of alternate views of land and community. In the journey from the libraries and coffeehouses of Boston, where these ideas first took root, to the desert expanses in Arizona, where they flowered in unexpected ways, I have been changed. I invite the reader to join me in identifying some of the more insidious forces that drive sprawl, and in searching for solutions that go beyond a prevailing and foreboding sense that sprawl is inevitable.

CHAPTER 1

THE RATIONAL SOCIETY

Heat waves roll off of the jet-black pavement, creating the illusion that streams of water cover the streets ahead. Stuck in a long line of cars, I watch as enormous truck tires appear to melt into the sweltering stretch of road before me. A mousy brown jeep trails behind, inching its way yet closer in an effort to squeeze into the small space beside me. We grow impatient. I slowly move forward as the light ahead turns green. The jeep restlessly shifts within the lane, waiting for the first opportunity to pass. Cars roll, accelerating and braking, in a tedious march forward.

Soon traffic begins to move more swiftly and, without delay, the jeep advances, disappearing into the distant heat waves. Dancing between lanes, we speed to our destinations, racing against each other in an attempt to achieve some unknown goal. With eyes fixed forward and jaw locked, I bound forth, past the ongoing stream of stores and strip malls, past the other cars cluttering the thoroughfare, rushing along with the pounding urban pace.

As I drive north, across Pima Road, all of the traffic, the businesses, the shops, the industry—all of the tension and the clamor of the city suddenly ceases. Expansive fields of kelly-green cotton unroll before me. I have arrived at the edge of the Salt River Community. Previously fixed on the concrete wall of stores lining the road, my eyes feel freed as they roam open land stretching out toward distant mountains. I pull over, get out of the car, and begin walking along the bed of the Salt River.

Towering sycamore trees extend into the big sky. Leaves crinkle as a slight breeze sweeps across the land. Wandering through groves of mesquite and cottonwoods that grow in the thickets

An aerial view of suburban sprawl in Phoenix.

along dry washes, I look for the river. They say that the under-current of the Salt River was once so powerful that anyone who attempted to swim across was swept to the bottom, never again to make it back to the top. Yet as I walk, the river never does appear. I learn that it was long ago diverted away from the Salt River Community and all that remains is cracked mud, sand, and silt. I stare out at the dry riverbed, devoid of its once lush vegetation, imagining it in its former majesty. Though redirected to feed the growing Phoenix metropolis, the Salt River shaped the Pima way of life. "We're River People," Loreen explains, "and we migrated from the ocean. That's where our name 'Authm' comes from." The Pimas trace their ancestry to the Hoo-hoogam,[1] which means "those who have gone." They received the name "Pima" when they responded *pimatch* ("I don't know") to a Spanish priest's questions. By around 1700, the Pimas occupied approximately seven "rancherias," spread seven to forty miles apart from each other. They lived in individual homes, separated by hundreds of acres of fields. To the Pimas, all life was intimately connected. Every being was a relative and land was something sacred, to be respected. The annual calendar was based on the corn crop, and songs, stories, and ceremonies were performed to honor the land and pray for the health of specific crops. From 2,230 to 3,050 Pimas existed in the Gila River Valley in 1700.[2]

The Dawes Act of 1887, implemented in the Salt River Community in 1911, restructured Pima life into five-, ten-, and twenty-acre tracts disrupting the village structure and communal approach to cultivating land. Under this system of land distribution, each generation received smaller plots until land became so fractionalized that land inheritances became too small to live on. By 1988, five-acre tracts had an average of 88 owners; ten- and twenty-acre tracts had an average of 289 owners.

Too many individuals owned the land tracts to allow each owner to have a physical piece of property. Instead, individuals own an "interest" in the property. When land is continually divided into allotments so that individuals have no physical land but rather an interest in it, the sense of place and space that once imbued the land with meaning is transformed. It became easier for Pima families to sell their interests to developers because the land was no longer perceived and experienced as alive, but rather was experienced more abstractly. Now land could be leased for outside private gain, thus placing a price on the land's worth and turning it into a quantifiable economic unit.

Today, the Salt River Community has leased out much of its western border so that this part of the reservation is no longer distinguishable from the rest of Phoenix. Their land is leased to commercial industry,[3] golf courses, a gaming casino, sand and gravel mining of the Salt River bed, and a landfill that serves the greater metropolitan area. Most notably, the Pavilion shopping area covers 146 acres with superstores, parking lots, and palm trees. Additionally, through a land exchange, nine miles of concrete highway (the Loop 101, also called the Pima Freeway) now traverses the reservation; it is part of the great system of highways designed to link all parts of Phoenix as it advances in all directions. Despite the pressure and incentive to develop land, 10,500 acres of agricultural land and 19,000 acres of open space still remain to distinguish the Salt River Community from the urbanization that has engulfed the region (Salt River Pima– Maricopa Indian Community, *General Development Plan: December, 1988*).

I return to my Nissan and drive toward the tribal government building. Alfalfa and cotton fields line the route and I wonder how the Salt River Community has managed to maintain as much agricultural land as it has. As in the case of Cave Creek, my interest in rural people who challenge the forces of development led me to the Salt River Community (population 4,877). There I observed two distinct value systems as they collided to produce, on the one hand, vast tracts of open space and farmland and, on the other hand, development indistinguishable from its sprawling neighbors. A look at this clash in value systems offers us some insight into how Western civilization's specific approach to nature[4] drives the growth society.

CULTURAL ORIENTATIONS TO LAND

Two key orientations to land distinguish traditional and modern societies and play critical roles in shaping the built environment. A symbolic and often religion-based relationship to land pervades traditional societies. Maintaining a symbolic relationship to the land means that the people of a particular society assign shared meaning to the land and its various parts. To traditional Pimas, landforms are physical manifestations of episodes that occurred during the Earth's creation and in the lives of the people. For example, according to the Pima creation story, Black Mountain was made from black gum that formed when one of the creators, Elder Brother, rolled in a vessel to escape floods. Stone Strike, a large lava mass in the eastern Santan Hills, is said to have formed when two women came upon a young man sleeping on a flat rock. To awaken the man, they tossed pebbles at him, until the pebbles amassed into a large mound. Andrew Gulliford (2000), professor of Southwest studies and history, has identified a typology of sacred sites common to traditional Native American communities. These include religious sites associated with oral traditions, trails and pilgrimage routes, traditional gathering areas, offering areas (altars and shrines), vision quest and other individual-use sites, group ceremonial sites where dances and sings sometimes take place, ancestral habitation sites, ceremonial rock art, individual burial and massacre sites, and observatories and calendar sites. Land is thus traditionally considered sacred and filled with meaning.

In contrast, rationalized relationships to land dominate modern industrial societies. Sociologist Max Weber posited that such societies are no longer governed by chance, feeling, emotions, and ethics as traditional societies are. Rather, modern societies are characterized by their rationality, efficiency, predictability, calculability, and control. Land in modern societies does not embody symbolic or religious meaning, but rather is viewed as a resource to be used and a commodity to be bought and sold. Sociologist George Ritzer (1993) has written that suburban communities, such as the Levittown of the early 1950s with its mass-produced housing, serve the rational society. Levitt and Sons built 17,447 homes within four years, creating an "instant community" of 75,000 people on former potato fields in New York. Construction workers performed specialized tasks as on an assembly line; however, rather than moving the product to the worker, the worker moved around the construction site and completed the same task on each home. All components of the homes were cut to fit—prefabricated—so that workers did not have to waste time measuring. Consequently, as one of the Levitts said, "Once the groundwork is down, houses go up boom, boom, boom" (Ritzer 1993:28). Ritzer concluded that "the result, of course, was a large number of nearly identical houses produced quickly and at low cost" (1993:28). Ultimately, such linear approaches to land render it divisible and easily arranged for efficient use and profit.

Although traditional and modern societies display differing orientations to the land, there is also considerable overlap. In some traditional societies, symbolic and religious relationships to the land are linked to functional and economic achievements. Additionally, dominant colonizing influences have affected traditional societies. Young people often embrace both traditional and modern orientations and apply differing orientations depending on the context. Traditional societies have also influenced industrial societies. Land is not always perceived in purely utilitarian ways in the industrialized world. For example, many countries legislate some form of recognition for indigenous sacred sites, although, as in the case with the American Indian Religious Freedom Act of 1978 (AIRFA), court tests of the law often fail to protect sacred sites and the protection of sites is often the product of intense political struggle. This is most recently illustrated in legal battles about using waste water for snowmaking on the San Francisco Peaks in northern Arizona. Ultimately, however, there are no "pure," single-faceted orientations to land, and cross-cultural influences blur any definitive categorization. Nevertheless, varying cultures display predominant tendencies that influence their relationship with land and it is these tendencies that serve as a focus in this discussion.

TRADITIONAL PIMA ORIENTATION TO LAND

The Pimas perceive themselves, other life, the land, and the planet as interconnected. "We don't see ourselves as the master of the land. It belongs to everybody and that includes the plants; that includes the animals, the sky above us," says Marcus, a Salt River Community member who is responsible for a cultural preservation project. Widening his eyes and staring out of his office window, Marcus continues, "It belongs to the birds. It belongs to the stars. In our view we are part of it and need to learn how to take care of it. We need to learn how to live with it."

Marcus explains: "The earth was made by spinning all over, not in just one direction, and there was nothing to hold it to keep it in place. So the creator said to the spider, 'I want you to spin your web between the earth and heaven.' And that's what the spider did. And he kept the earth in its place and allowed it to spin on its axis."

Anthropologist Frank Russell (1908) has retold the Pima creation story for a Western audience. By tradition, the story, customarily orally transmitted to sons, takes four days to tell. While impossible to record all aspects of the creation story, highlighting some points, as paraphrased from Russell's account, offers insight into how land maintains meaning and symbolic resonance for the people.

THE PIMA CREATION STORY
In the beginning was nothing. Gathering ages of darkness collected into a great mass forming the spirit of Earth Doctor. He

Pima Freeway. This image shows how the Pima "Man in the Maze symbol" is incorporated into the freeway structure in an effort to be "culturally sensitive." "The legend of the 'Man in the Maze' helps children understand the meaning of life. The maze depicts experiences and choices we make in our journey through life.... In the middle of the maze are found a person's dreams and goals. Legend says when we reach the center, the Sun God is there to greet us, bless us, and pass us into the next world." (Salt River Pima–Maricopa Indian Community, "The Community.")

drifted. To ground himself, Earth Doctor took dust from his chest and flattened it into a cake. He thought forth a creosote bush. Every time Earth Doctor stood up he fell. However, on the fourth time, he stood still and began to sing the rest of the world into existence. He sang a termite into existence that worked upon the Earth until the Earth reached its present state. Earth Doctor made a sky to cover the Earth. The sky was shaped like a Pima roundhouse.

The Earth was still unsteady, so Earth Doctor made gray spider, who spun a web around the earth and sky, connecting the edges. After the Earth was steadied, he made a dish and poured water into it. Water turned to ice and Earth Doctor threw it North. The shining ice became the sun. The sun rose and slid back down again. So Earth Doctor threw the sun to the West. It rose and slid down. Earth Doctor threw the sun to the South. It rose and slid down. When Earth Doctor threw the sun East, it rose until it reached a great height and then sank into the West.

Darkness fell into deep blackness. Earth Doctor threw ice to the North and it formed the moon. The moon also rose and sunk until Earth Doctor threw it to the East where it rises today. When the moon sunk, the night became very dark. So Earth Doctor took water into his mouth and sprayed it into the sky to make the stars. He threw ashes onto his walking stick and drew his stick across the sky to make the Milky Way.

Earth Doctor formed human beings out of clay. However, human overpopulation led to war. Feeling he must relieve their distress, Earth Doctor took his staff to the sky and pulled the sky down, destroying all humans. Earth Doctor went through a hole in the Earth and came out the other side.

Moon gave birth to Coyote, who came to the land where the Pima people now live. Earth gave birth to Elder Brother, who shortened human lives so that they would not overrun the Earth. Nevertheless, Elder Brother and Earth Doctor were unsatisfied with human beings and spread great floods upon the Earth.

Coyote was carried south by a drifting log and Earth Doctor escaped the floods by enclosing himself in a reed. Elder Brother rolled along until he came to rest by the Colorado River. Black gum collected from his vessel and formed Black Mountain, which is still there today.

Earth Brother, Earth Doctor, and Coyote continued to create new beings. Earth Doctor tried to sink into the Earth. However, when he was halfway down, Elder Brother jumped in and tried to catch him. While trying to hold Earth Doctor, Elder Brother's hands got covered with dirt and blood. When he shook his hands, blood sprinkled all over the Earth. This is what causes illness and disease among us now. Elder Brother and Coyote, now in

*control of the Earth, created many other beings, including four
tribes, one of which was the Pima tribe.*

The story continues. However, from this brief selection, we can
see how important such things as the four directions, the earth,
moon, sun and stars, and particular mountains and landmasses
are to the Pimas. We see how certain structures, like the traditional roundhouse, were modeled after nature's forms. As with
other indigenous peoples, the Pimas identify their current land
as land that they have lived on since the beginning of human
existence. The creation story gets integrated into the daily lives
of the people and is used to interpret present-day events.

As a child, Marcus's grandfather used to run after planes with
his friends, wondering what they were and how they could fly.
"To my grandfather, all those planes flying out there were cutting
the spiders' webs. There were too many of them," says Marcus.
"Now people are starting to realize that you can't disrespect the
earth—hairspray and all that. With all the developments, people
are not having a respect for the land. Some day the earth will
catch on fire and start burning and everything will be swallowed
up." This orientation to the land as alive and sacred stands in
stark contrast to the dominant modern industrial model that
views land as a resource with a market value.

In the late 1980s the Arizona Department of Transportation
sought "undeveloped land" to build the Loop 101 Freeway.
"Outsiders don't realize this land belongs to somebody. They
just see it as bare land," says Tony, a middle-aged Pima man
whose leathery hands indicate a lifetime of agricultural work.
Tony explains that the land is anything but barren. "The land is
alive and the dead who have been unearthed through developing
the freeway are angered and restless." Many believe that the
hardships they now face are a result of angry ancestors whose
resting spots have been disturbed through development. Reburial ceremonies seek to rectify the imbalance and bring respect
back to their ancestors and to the land.

I sit with June under an expansive shade tree, trying to keep cool in the 110° F heat. Bare-footed, June seems cool and relaxed in her white t-shirt and jeans. I am sweating profusely, not used to the extreme heat. June tells me, "They think the land is just there and that we weren't using it for what they thought we should be using if for. So they thought, 'let's put it to use.' This is not our way."

Traditional Pima views on land and nature are inconsistent with urbanization, so even tribal officials who tend to support "economic development" are quick to acknowledge that development must respect the Pima culture and the land. "We don't want wall-to-wall concrete; we want to see some open space," says Rose, who directs Salt River Community development policy decisions. "We want to be able to see the mountains. We want to be able to see the farmland, yet generate income for families."

Whereas Pima cosmology is inconsistent with urbanization, leading to comprehensive community efforts to preserve large areas of open space and farmland, "civilized" Western ideas of nature fuel our sprawling suburbs. Western ideas, rooted in a Judeo-Christian tradition, view human beings as distinctly separate from and in control of the rest of nature. "Multiply and fill the earth and subdue it; you are masters of the fish and birds and all the animals," reads Genesis 1:28. In Genesis, the first human beings, Adam and Eve, are eventually expelled from their birthplace, the Garden of Eden. Whereas traditional indigenous cultures trace their present homeland to the first moments of human creation, Westerners do not live on the same land that they attribute to their human origins. As a result, Westerners have a different relationship to the land.

With the dawn of modern science in the seventeenth century, the people of modern industrial nations began to view nature as not only distinct from human beings but also as an object. As an object in a burgeoning industrial society, land was viewed in relation to its uses, so land remaining "unused" was deemed

Agriculture on leased Pima land. Outside businesses lease land from the Salt River Community for agriculture.

"wasted." Sprawl can be thought of as a rather efficient model for using up land.

June and I continue talking as we walk amidst the cotton crop that borders her home. Standing among acres of cotton, I look in one direction and find my eyes take a linear and direct path over miles of red roofs that form a tightly packed lattice and stretch out toward distant mountains. Looking in the other direction, my eyes seem to pause before focusing on some vague movement that I sense among the desert scrub. A jackrabbit peeks up from behind a bush and then ducks behind another. After another pause, my eyes drift freely before resting upon the horizon. My senses offer a direct and corporeal understanding of how these two opposing belief systems shape land development. A look at the history of modern science and nineteenth-century efforts to plan the modern "rational" city offers us additional insight into the mindset that has resulted in our sprawling suburbs.

RATIONALIZED ORIENTATION TO LAND

In *Meditations*, Rene Descartes (1641) established the mind/body dualism that helped set the stage for modern science and the consequent objectification of nature that drives sprawl as well as all other environmentally destructive activity. In response to the skepticism of the age (epitomized by Montaigne's notion that if the senses deceive us, how do we know anything?),[5] Descartes held that, although the senses are subject to deception, the mind could establish certain fundamental truths. "Cogito, ergo sum." I think, therefore I am. The very fact that I can think about my own existence proves that I am something. The mind can discern fundamental truths, but in the absence of clarity must refrain from passing judgments. Knowledge may thus be objectified and may exist separately from the sensory world.

Descartes' mind/body dualism, with its recognition of the self as objective observer, epitomized the Age of Reason and the subsequent Scientific Revolution. Indeed, Descartes solidified the subject/object split and ushered in what we now term the "modern condition," characterized by the radical disassociation between subjects and objects, a flat exterior world composed of individual objects that we may isolate and directly observe and understand. Newton's laws of motion[6] drew on this subject/object split to create a coherent theory of reality, a theory that could explain all of the workings of the universe. We now define the physics of the modern era as "Newtonian Physics" because it offers a complete theory of physical reality.

The Scientific Revolution, assisted by the Age of Reason, Descartes' mind/body duality and his notions of inert and passive matter, as well as Newton's science of mechanics,[7] transformed the world into a deterministic universe whereby an objective reality existed. This objective reality was based on the assertion that matter was passive, inert, and made of discrete solid particles. If the future of every particle and its velocity could be mapped out, then the future of the universe could be precisely predicted. This idea took the very "life" out of our attempts to understand existence. Existence now consisted of solid, lifeless particles of matter.

City planners based their projects on the unspoken lifelessness of the material world. They rose to prominence in the Newtonian world of the late nineteenth century—a world viewed as both predictable and controllable. Planners sought to apply rational scientific understanding to the problems of market-driven haphazard development of the modern industrial city. In response to such overdevelopment, characterized by William H. Wilson (1983) as vast "seas of unplanning," they focused on the plotting of streets along the "grid," first developed by Thomas Jefferson in 1784.[8] Whereas Newton viewed the mapping out of all particles and their velocities as the key to understanding the universe, planners viewed the mapping out of the city along a grid as the key for understanding, controlling, and organizing the growth of the city. Yet, control of city growth did not curb that growth. Early planning efforts continued to focus on rapid development and on how to turn quick profits. As writer and humanist Lewis Mumford wrote, "Such plans fitted nothing but a quick parceling of the land, a quick conversion of farmsteads into real estate, and a quick sale. . . . Urban land, too, now became a mere commodity, like labor: its market value expressed its only value"

(1961:422). The city grid did not curb development, but simply made it more efficient.

Yet city planning, with its emphasis on scientific efficiency, emerged precisely in response to the problems associated with such market-driven development. Urban planning professor Donald Krueckeberg has written that "enterprise alone bred chaos. Cooperation for efficient development was essential to the survival of city life" (1983:6). With a focus on urban renewal and beautification (such as introducing parks to the colorless crowded cities of the Industrial Era), planning had a strong social reform agenda. Its emphasis on scientific efficiency came as a savior's promise against a variety of threats intrinsic to the nineteenth century, the most fundamental of which was the threat of epidemic yellow fever, making the implementation of plans "for the common good" a matter of "human survival" (Krueckeberg 1983).

The history of planning is a history fraught with struggles between market forces that emphasize rapid development and planning reforms that focus on social equity, civic beauty, and more recently ecological concerns. Over the course of the twentieth century, planning narrowed its vision from the whole city to the development of individual communities. By the 1980s planning-as-project and planning-as-real-estate-development became standard practice.

Planning often cannot deliver on its original social reform visions. Planner Mary Hommann has illustrated this difficulty with an analogy:

> City planning as constituted in America is like a tiny pilot fish swimming alongside a great shark. The economic system, the real estate business, home rule statutes, financial markets, political parties, government agencies, the labor movement, the corporate world, the interstate highway network—these, and others, are the great sharks of modern life. American city planning is too insignificant to do more than flutter alongside one or another of these great sharks and try to look intelligent. (1993:142–43)

Today, the market-driven power located in the hands of developers and the real estate industry make it as challenging as ever for planners to realize reform ideals. Compromise, and more often conformity to the developer and real estate plans, becomes necessary.

City planners of today value good planning, by which they mean *how* developments are planned. Planners focus on design elements, architectural design, and the acquisition of technical expertise (geographical information systems and management, cartography, and remote sensing). Planners also seek to maintain community character and open space insofar as open space provides what they call a sense of "continuity." In designing the well-planned community of the twenty-first century, planners' visions rarely conflict with developers' interests.

Ultimately, growth may now be planned, or scientifically managed, but the rate of growth continues to increase. Although we may have a better handle on disease and social maladies, the act of "planning for growth" opens up doors for further damage to ecological systems. This makes us vulnerable to more and different types of diseases and social problems than the planning industry originally sought to address.[9]

Who Benefits?

From the perspective of planning for growing communities, the Phoenix freeway network appears as one attempt within a larger endeavor to grow responsibly. Rather than leading to chaotic development, the freeway system links communities, creating a connective tissue that integrates the metropolitan area. And yet this approach literally paves over land, going against the alternative views of those who, like the Pimas, struggle to maintain a rural land base.

Suburban sprawl arises from an ideological framework that perceives the individual as distinct from and in control of nature. In viewing land as subservient to our wants and needs, we have chopped it up into smaller and smaller pieces for the purposes of efficient management and ownership. "Growth makes economies successful. The Valley should embrace it, not fear it or rein it in. 'Sprawl' is not an evil force. The key for the future is to *manage growth efficiently*," advises popular economist David Birch (*The Phoenix Business Journal*, October 8, 1999, my emphasis). Only individuals with access to the dominant power structures really benefit, at least economically, from this ideological framework. The poor, inner-city minorities of South Phoenix, find their community devastated in the wake of sprawl. Here, 150 lots remain vacant as more money goes to the out-skirts of the metropolis rather than to revitalizing the inner city (Lincoln Institute 2003). The poor all over the United States find their communities in a state of abandonment or as the dumping grounds for the better-off who would rather not place waste incinerators and industrial facilities in their own communities and who have access to the decision-making processes that pre-vent this from happening.[10]

Indigenous communities engulfed by sprawl find their land transformed as the pressures to lease land to outside forces, as in the case of the Salt River Community, make maintaining the integrity of their land base a continual challenge. All 562 feder-ally recognized Native American tribes have been limited to reservations typically composed of the most impoverished land in the country, generally not large enough to sustain traditional farming or grazing practices in these times. Reservation land is often further divided into a checkerboard configuration with small parcels of land maintained by the tribe or tribal members and adjoining parcels leased to industry. Leasing land is often the most direct approach tribes have to sustain themselves, as the small allotments of reservation land cannot otherwise support an entire tribe.

In essence, the suburban sprawl that rises out of our "rational society," a society that views nature and ourselves as essentially separate, primarily serves those with access to power, reinforc-

The rational model of land. In this image we can see the contrast between
the undeveloped desert and the rational model of land. Suburban sprawl
renders land "useable" by partitioning land into discreet sections.

ing their power and drawing resources away from those less integrated into the dominant power structures. Who benefits from
the dominant growth model? How do the stories that we tell ourselves and the assumptions that we make support the growth
society? These are the types of questions that we must ask if we
are to begin to understand how dominant perceptions and ideological frameworks support sprawl and to challenge these ways
of thinking.

CHAPTER 2

CULTURAL PRODUCTIONS OF SPACE AND TIME

Flying over the Sonoran Desert for the first time, I found myself captivated by the vast stretches of land, by the understated layers of reds, oranges, yellows, and browns, the tapestry of color, texture, and shadow that forms the subtle beauty of the desert. Land seemed endless and my mind meandered through intricate patterns over the many miles. Soon great rocky ridges appeared and I was startled to see that the land no longer rolled on in its hypnotic way. Now I saw a checkerboard with geometric boxes—some green, some brown, some with little red dots. My mind could no longer roam but was limited to the confines of the little boxes that covered the landscape.

As we descended into Phoenix, I realized that the green boxes were farms. I saw that the brown boxes were scraped desert, cleared of foliage to prepare for future housing developments. The squares with the little red dots emerged as the red clay tile roofs of countless miles of homes. The checkerboard order that characterizes Phoenix as well as other modern American cities arises from the rational society of the nineteenth and twentieth centuries.

Social scientists have observed[1] that various cultural groups use and experience space differently. While human senses perceive space, our cultural frameworks define and organize space. Others have analyzed[2] how cultural frameworks define and organize time. Taken together, examination of the cultural productions of time and space offer us further insight into how development proceeds in the desert.

More specifically, an analysis of the shifts from traditional to modern industrialized societies helps us to understand smaller scale shifts in development among communities in the Sonoran Desert. As noted in Chapter 1, land in rationalized societies is viewed as a commodity to be bought and sold. So the rational orientation to land prompts us to construct time and space into linear, manageable pieces—organized to optimize efficiency, predictability, calculability, and control.

Sociologist Eviatar Zerubavel (1991) has elaborated on cultural practices that have rational approaches to time and space. Zerubavel (who uses the term "rigid" to describe what I am calling "rationalized") observes that rigid orientations to time and space seek to avoid anything that is unclear and ambiguous. The rigid mind seeks clarity, boundaries, and sharply delineated categories. Space is quantifiable and viewed as coordinates on a grid. Time is perceived linearly. The basic rhythm of modern life, planned and efficient, moves to the order of the clock. A rational orientation to space and time is steeped in a Newtonian science of mechanics and Cartesian mind/body split where matter is viewed as passive, inert, and composed of discrete particles. Thus, private property and privacy with their clear physical boundaries and rigid social structures (illustrated by the many clearly defined rules of homeowners' associations) are highly valued features of rationalized societies.

In contrast, "The fuzzy mind . . . invokes a world made up of vague essences fading gradually into one another," writes Zerubavel. "Instead of clear-cut dimensions, it highlights ambiguity" (1991:115). In societies where space and time are malleable and fluid, land is not divisible and quantifiable. Most traditional societies are nonlinear and organized according to direct needs as they arise in the community. Building patterns are often cyclical as determined by the rhythms of the lunar or solar calendar. The Zunis, for example, build new homes in preparation for the Shalako, messengers from the spirit world, who appear between the winter solstice and the full moon. The fluid orientation to land is nature-directed. This orientation confers a sense of mystery—a sense of ambiguity and value for the unknown.

Traditional societies do structure space and time.[3] However, their structures are nonlinear and not based on efficiency, predictability, calculability, and control. Societies that maintain an extreme fluid orientation may also subject individuals to unjust social arrangements. Since fluidity is honored above more rigid structures, there is more opportunity for such biases as favoritism, discrimination, and any range of inequalities to gain fertile ground. Furthermore, as discussed in Chapter 1, many traditional societies comfortably maintain a rational orientation part of the time while participating in the fluid rites and traditions of their culture at other times. Thus, these cultural orientations should be viewed as patterns or tendencies and not firm rules. Even so, cultural patterns and tendencies, orientations to reality, shape choices made and directions taken. Ultimately, a rationalized approach to time and space shapes the growth society.

This chapter examines the relationship between cultural productions of time and space and "dwelling"—how homes are oriented within communities and how we live upon the land. The use of the term "dwelling" derives from Tim Ingold's (2000) emphasis on using a "dwelling perspective." In defining dwelling, Ingold asks us to understand relations between human beings as not simply "social relations" but also as "ecological relations." I will look at how three communities' approaches to time and space influence their dwellings. I begin by examining how Pima elders' traditional approaches to time and space shaped their community and how movement away from this worldview toward a more rational orientation has led the next generation of Salt River Pimas to lease their land to commercial development.

Pima Elders in the Salt River
Pima-Maricopa Indian Community

In the 1870s and 1880s, hundreds of irrigation companies sought to "reclaim the West," to make the desert habitable and to gain quick wealth. Yet the daunting challenges and cost of building dams large enough to supply a year-round flow of water led to the demise of the irrigation companies. In the 1890s a series of natural catastrophes and the failure of private irrigation efforts inspired the Federal Irrigation Movement. Federal Reclamation Acts thus enabled settlement of the American West, and one reclamation project, the Salt River Project, enabled the settlement and growth of Phoenix.

Prior to the Salt River Project, the Gila and its tributaries, the Salt and Verde Rivers, wandered through the arid Sonoran Desert and eventually evaporated. However, after the Salt River Project redirected the river for effective irrigation, water became expensive and the Pimas could no longer afford to farm their own land. Donald Bahr, who spent more than twenty years working with Pima singers, has written that "the community stopped its farming between the 1940s and 60s, but not from lack of water. Rather, as Paul [a Pima Singer] sees it, the reason was that people could not pay for the water from a new irrigation system that was built for them" (Bahr et al. 1997:10–11). Prior to the reclamation project, an acre of desert had been worth five or ten dollars. Now it was worth fifty times the original amount. Farmers sold out to wealthy speculators, who essentially took over the Salt River Project, and an entire way of life was transformed (Reisner 1993:117). While the Pimas still consider themselves agricultural people and maintain an agricultural land base, much of that land is leased out to non-Pima farmers who can afford to irrigate the land.

Damming the Salt River to accommodate a growing Phoenix population transformed the relationship between the Pimas and the land. For elders in the Salt River Community, time and space

Damming the Salt River. This photograph illustrates the diversion of water by the Arizona Central Project from dams fed by the Colorado River and its tributaries (including the Salt River) into the surrounding Phoenix metropolitan area. Water that once went directly to the Salt River Community no longer runs through the community.

drastically changed when, as one elder explained, "they turned off the water." As I listened to their stories, I began to acquire not only a sense of how damming the river has transformed the area but also insight into how a traditional orientation toward time and space shaped how the Pimas once lived on the land. Through listening to their stories, I learned how the traditional orientation of the Pima elders became disrupted and the effect this disruption has had on the community.

Elders paint an idyllic picture of their childhood world—a timeless world where one's needs were directly met by the fruit of the land. "There was plum trees, peach trees, pecan trees—it was always shady around there," Pam, grandmother of six, recalls. "We lived in little frame houses with a lot of grass and meadow. We had this big old pond where the animals drank and the wastewater went. And all kinds of birds and a lot of trees. Of course we ate the plums, and whatever was in season—[fruit from] the orange trees, grapefruit trees. It was a good place to live."

Land was part of a timeless fabric of family life in the Salt River Community. Families lived on the same piece of land for generations. For many generations Helen's family lived in a home on the other side of a five-acre field from where she now lives. A fire burned the home down and her family rebuilt across the field; however, Helen still believes that she belongs across the field with her ancestors. Her "new home," more than twenty years old when we spoke, was misplaced and "so far away" from where she felt she belonged. Helen appeared out of sync with the rhythm of the "new" land—land untouched by the generations who came before her.[4]

A strong sense of the rhythm of the land permeates elders' stories. Pam's story highlights how the Pima sense of time was remarkably different from the contemporary rhythm of daily life. "One time my parents brought home a big old mountain tortoise. And they went wood hunting, they used to go way out there where Fountain Hills is, that's where they used to go to get wood. They brought this big old tortoise home." A faraway look crosses Pam's dark eyes as she remembers. "The tortoise was neat. In summertime he used to let me ride on his back and he used to take me to the outhouse because I didn't always wear shoes and then he'd take me back."

The trips Pam took to the outhouse on her large mountain tortoise made me cognizant of the cultural value of time. I found it hard to imagine anyone choosing to take a slow-moving tortoise to the bathroom in today's rush to make such inconveniences irrelevant—after all, time is of the essence and we cannot "waste time."

The elders also offered me insight into their perception of space. Pima elders recall the importance of seeing their sacred mountains and buttes. I learned from their accounts how important it was to look into the distance, a view now restricted for

Traditional Pima home made of saguaro and mud.

some by miles of housing developments. June, grandmother and administrator for the tribal court, remembers:

> We didn't have electricity but we had a nice home. No phones. If you really wanted to call somebody we walked to somebody's house. I don't know how they always knew, but if we wanted somebody to come over to the house, we'd flash a mirror over there and they'd come. I remember they used to do that, my grandfather, my uncle. Because then you were able to see far. But now you really can't see too much because there's a lot of homes now. The air. It's more dirtier. I know when it's going to be winter or fall. It's more dirtier and you can't see as far. It disturbs me because I can't see the mountains.

Communication through the use of flashing mirrors indicates an entirely different use of space. The flashing mirror spanned space and connected Pima families. There was no need to bridge thousands of miles with phone wires and other technologies because the entire community was also connected through social dances and songs for holidays, harvests, and birthdays, and

Most homes in the Salt River Community look like this image—small HUD homes surrounded by large shade trees.

transformative dances and songs to cure illness, foretell rain, and learn the location of animals. To this day, many Pima households do not have phones, although many of these traditional means of communication are no longer practiced.

Damming the water brought electricity to the reservation and changed the rhythms of day-to-day life. Electricity transformed the meaning of day and night. Through the diversion of the Salt River to feed Phoenix, the riverbed dried up and so did the community's lush land. The ditches devoted to swimming, bathing, and drinking became polluted, as did the air.

The elders remember a time when the land flourished, providing fruit, animals, drinking water, and wood. Traveling to the water offered a day's adventure. Time and space were holistic experiences, tied to the direct needs of the community. Yet this perception of time and space was violently disrupted by the construction of the dam. The water stopped. Trees disappeared. Pima families could no longer afford to water their crops. Now supplied with the water from the Salt River, Phoenix began

One of the mansions built after sale of land to the Arizona Department of Transportation to build the freeway.

"sprawling" toward the Salt River Community, encasing sacred mountains in smog and filling the deep night sky with light.

MASTER-PLANNED COMMUNITIES

Much of this expanding development has come in the form of master-planned communities first developed in the Phoenix metropolitan area in the 1960s when Scottsdale city officials sought to create a "General Master Plan." In contrast to subdivisions, which consist of multiple housing units developed in the hope that shopping, commercial centers, schools, and parks will rise around them, master-planned communities incorporate countless amenities into their development plans.

As opposed to the sporadic growth of subdivision communities, developers claim that master-planned communities are more responsible. Yet such communities play a key role in creating sprawl, for they transform large areas of land, often outside of the city limits, into housing developments. They exemplify

Garreau's (1988) notion of edge cities as they incorporate large retail centers and other industry into communities on the city's outskirts. Master-planned communities could potentially alleviate traffic and pollution, as all the necessities of daily life exist within the community; however, since most master-planned communities extend away from the city center, residents who work in the inner city have long commutes on crowded highways. The master-planned community ultimately guides development in the desert. As Tim Rogers (2005), a Phoenix agent for Century21, wrote, "Recent estimates show that over 80% of new home construction permits issued by Valley building developments were issued for homes in Master-Planned Communities!"

Master-planned communities, which epitomize the contemporary orientation with its control of time and space, produce a flatland that is literal as well as metaphorical. No irregular surface interrupts the perfectly horizontal lay of the land in dozens of communities observed. Miles of California-style stucco walls separate these self-enclosed communities from bordering neighborhoods, roads, and land. Elaborate showcase entrances welcome the newcomer and offer us the first taste of how time and space are thoughtfully controlled so as to offer us an illusion— an illusion of the desert as an entrance ticket to the American Dream (see Chapter 3).

A walk through Del Webb's Anthem Parkside on a bright spring morning illustrates how master-planned communities construct space and time to effect a different kind of dwelling and maintain a rational orientation. I enter Anthem Park, located forty-five miles north of Phoenix and surrounded by desert, and the first thing my eyes fall upon is water rippling over a large wall with "Anthem" engraved into it. The sound of splashing water makes me feel that I have entered a water park. The wide four lanes of Gulivan Parkway encircle the community and mimic the wide, open expanse of the Sonoran Desert. However, the desert's varied contours, scraggly brush and dust, that only eight years ago defined this area, have been replaced by

Anthem's controlled landscape. Here crushed imitation rocks line walkways; real desert rock apparently lacks rich enough tones. Authentic rock is perhaps too random in texture. In Anthem I do not see the burned or misshaped saguaro limbs found on the other side of the community's walls. Here perfect saguaro cacti stretch their strong arms into the deep blue sky.

This is the desert as it should be. This is the desert I recognized from advertisements, a place where one can escape the everyday bustle of the city. Huge homes stuffed into small plots line the streets. Some display miniature washes with smooth river rock. The "real" washes, the "original" desert, exist on the opposite side of the walls that surround and delineate Anthem Park. A sign reads, "Wash Out Area," an unintended reminder that the desert is not a benign place and even our constructions cannot control the power of a flash flood.

While driving through the Anthem community, I cannot see the desert that lay behind the stucco walls but for occasional glimpses. The positioning of the streets, lower than the building elevation, has the effect of sinking the driver below the property lines so that all I can see are Anthem homes and blue sky. The Sonoran Desert is nowhere in sight unless one stands on a roof and looks out past miles of rooftops. Anthem tells us: *this* is the desert; this is what matters; this is what is real.

Yet through its conservation program, Anthem works to respect the native trees and desert land. The conservation program focuses on replanting saguaros, refraining from building past a certain level on surrounding mountains, and painting homes in the muted colors of the desert. Developers seek to offer residents a feel for the desert removed from its actual dirt and sand. The problem is, even while preserving certain aspects of the desert, a master-planned community like Anthem controls the environment to such a degree that the desert itself becomes a mere convenience. As a planner involved in Anthem's development states, "The Sonoran Desert is an amenity from a development perspective."

While acknowledging efforts to preserve certain aspects of the desert, I ponder: What does paving over and redesigning the desert for the needs of a master-planned community actually do to the desert ecosystem? How does building forty-five miles away from the city center affect all the land in between? Invariably, this land becomes prime real estate for more development, encouraging what is commonly called "leapfrog development." In order to increase profit, developers "leap" to less valuable land, which is not adjacent to already developed areas, thus further developing into the desert.

Anthem residents engage in a range of activities: A man prunes his trees; a young family plays baseball using palm trees for bases; individuals go to the Community Center where they play in the 400,000 gallon "Big Splash Water Park," attend barbeques, have picnics, and partake of numerous other recreational activities. These images mirror the cartooned icons sketched into the sides of the Anthem vans, lining the tiles in the sidewalks, and imprinted on all the brochures: images of a bike, lawn chair, apple on a book, baseball glove and ball, wooden toy train, picnic basket with red and white checkered blanket, and watermelon slice. In this way Anthem makes the intimate experiences of life, a picnic, or a moment in the sun, "public," and sells the promise of a life fully lived in the very floor tiles that line a walkway and on the sides of vans.

Residents in master-planned communities do not seem to mind the controlled environment. Mary, a graduate student in an environmental studies program, explains that she can help shape her community's conservation program through her work with the homeowners' association. "The controlled environment of a master-planned community is one that also controls pollution and the way people live on the land," she tells me. "I would rather live here than any other place in the Valley. It's a place where I can minimize my effect." Through incorporating energy and water-efficient features into her home, Mary believes she does her best to live in an environmentally sensitive way. David also feels that the master-planned community offers a better way of life. "I know my neighbors. Where I used to live, no one knew each other, now we see each other at the pool and at the park." When I ask David, a thirty-eight-year-old business executive, what he thinks about the development of desert land, he tells me that all this land is going to be developed anyway. "It's inevitable, so I might as well live in a community that is at least trying to conserve and live in a better way."

Many choose to live in master-planned communities because they offer a range of recreational choices and provide residents with opportunities to conserve the environment. Residents speak about their communities as places that maintain a small-town feeling in the midst of exquisite beauty. There is a romanticization of the "local" that echoes back to a different era when communities had more defined boundaries and depended more fully upon themselves. Yet "local" loses much of its original meaning in an age where mega-corporations border these outlying communities, supplying them with goods and services from a global market. While residents identify with the small-town local feeling they get in the planned community, the dependence on large global corporations to supply basic needs conceals a reality that is often at odds with the ecological values they hold. For example, bordering Anthem Parkside lies a string of corporations such as Safeway Grocery, Ace Hardware, McDonald's, Walgreen's, Starbucks—all recent additions to this part of the Sonoran Desert, all requiring vast resources to run, and all capitalizing on the lack of resources endemic to life in the desert. The controlled environment of master-planned communities, furthermore, gets equated with a sense that we also control our human impact on the land. This may be so in certain limited ways; however, living in communities so far removed from the city center encourages leapfrog development and is precisely what perpetuates sprawl.

As I drive out of one community, I see a truck advertising the company name, "All About Water and Ice." Yes, I think to

This billboard advertised a new master-planned community, Anthem, forty-five miles north of Phoenix. The land that this billboard stood upon was undeveloped until 1999 when Del Webb built the Anthem Community. The billboard depicts the recreational area, although that is a very small part of the master plan—the land is now filled in with miles of homes tightly packed together.

myself, it is all about water and ice here. The desert has been transformed and I have been transported to a paradise where the sun always shines, it never rains, and yet water appears everywhere. A controlled and carefully constructed reality transforms time and space so that we may escape "nature" and live in simulations of our own making.

French philosopher Jean Baudrillard drew upon the desert geology of the Southwest to visit the "mental deserts" of America, mental deserts that sprawling Southwestern cities epitomize. By "mental deserts" Baudrillard alluded to how Americans tend to see only the surface of things, seeing land as useless, for example, and creating value out of uselessness while overlooking the complex desert ecology that such land supports. He presented a form of "social desertification" where American culture

This image of a master-planned community, located in the I-17 corridor north of Phoenix and south of Anthem, demonstrates how space is linearly constructed.

ironically reproduces the arid, spacious forms of the desert geology. "There is a sort of miracle in the insipidity of *artificial paradises*, so long as they achieve the greatness of an entire (un)culture. In America, space lends a sense of grandeur even to the insipidity of the suburbs and 'funky towns'. The desert is everywhere, preserving insignificance" (Baudrillard 1989:8).

Baudrillard's cynical view of America crystallizes through my observations of master-planned communities. Time and space flatten out in these places of hyper-reality where the dream replaces reality. The model itself becomes the truth and we find a linear one-dimensional plane in which superficiality is glorified. Welcome to paradise, and don't forget to "review the guidelines that provide for a sense of community and neighborhood" (Sherman 2002:5). That reminder appears in Del Webb's Anthem Parkside Activity Guide. Everything is arranged and controlled in the master-planned community.

CAVE CREEK, ARIZONA

In contrast to the controlled order of master-planned communities, many Cave Creek residents seek to maintain a symbolic and more traditional orientation, viewing land as sacred and filled with mystery. John, a leader of Friends of Spur Cross, whose sandy blond hair seems to blend in with the desert sands, extends his arm out across the land and remembers what it was like the first time he came to this area. John highlights this syncretic orientation when speaking of the "irrational pull" that drew him to the area:

> For some reason as we came up to Cave Creek, I don't know why, I turned right on Spur Cross and just bee-lined to the end of Spur Cross Road to Spur Cross Ranch. And I came over that ridge, like I was drawn there and there was this panorama. And I thought, "This is gorgeous." Then I just started bringing my horses to go horseback riding up there. I felt part of a continuum that's been there for 1500 years. You know I could almost see Native Americans milling about, kids running around. For some reason I thought I was supposed to have been there.

Also taking a more symbolic approach to nature, Becky, grandmother and long-time resident of Cave Creek, discusses her intuitive connection with the land:

> I feel a matriarchal sense comes through me that says, "This shall not occur." Like a female panther protective thing. Like a panther, I'm pretty mellow until somebody threatens my children or something else that shouldn't be threatened. And that's a very short list of things that people can't mess with. One is my children and the other is sacred spaces. And some part of me kicks into high gear at that point.

The eloquent earth-centered language that so many Cave Creek residents speak, heartfelt, poetic, and passionate, is nonetheless couched within a rationalized time/space orientation. Hence, many call for a reunion with Mother Earth's rhythms while simultaneously maintaining linear assumptions about time and space. For example, in Cave Creek the very mention of land appears to go hand-in-hand with zoning. Zoning, the arrangement of land into sections reserved for different purposes (residence or business), like the city grid, renders space divisible and ultimately consumable. Although I never brought up the word "zone," all Cave Creek residents mentioned zoning at some point in our discussions. Property rights advocates tended to think that the town's 2.5-acre zoning laws provided plenty of space for native habitat. Environmentalists tended to critique this zoning, feeling that homes should be built with even more space between them. One couple discussed the economic ramifications of the town's "low-density zoning" as inhibiting lower-income families from settling into the area. Yet, whatever their position, zoning organized the debate around development. (See Chapter 5 for more on the property rights versus environmentalist debate.)

Zoning also organized perceptions of space. Whereas environmentalists perceived a development like Red Dog Ranch with its one-acre zoning as an eyesore and environmental disaster, property rights advocates considered it a beautiful residential community offering plenty of open space. Whatever their position on zoning, the *zone* and one's relationship to land *as zoned* defines discussion about development. The zone determines how much and what is deemed "responsible," despite many residents' desires to move toward a more traditional symbolic orientation. In this way, discourse on zoning relegates space into the rational realm, divisible, and based on exchange value.

Rationalized notions of time also order reality in Cave Creek. My experience with scheduling interviews provides a subtle example of this. I easily set up interviews with Cave Creek residents by calling them on a weekend and setting up times to meet the following weekend. Cave Creek residents, like most

Americans, view time linearly. Thus, it was "natural" to set up interviews for a specific time of day that suited individuals' schedules.

Our entrenchment in a linear world becomes blatantly clear when we interact with individuals from cultures different from our own. When I called Salt River Pima residents for interviews I found it virtually impossible to schedule meetings. Individuals would tell me, "Why don't you come and then we'll see?" I did not really know what that meant. If I made the three-hour trip from my home in Flagstaff to the Salt River Community, how would I find them? At what time? If Community members did not want to participate, would the trip be a "waste of time"? I was utterly baffled by such responses to my requests for interviews. In several cases, individuals who had been recommended to me did not have a phone. How could I find them? After numerous attempts to schedule interviews, I realized that another approach was necessary— many Pimas did not view time linearly. Perhaps time is more circular in the Pima worldview. It wraps upon itself and so if I miss someone or something today, it will circle back to me another day. Space was also a more fluid concept. I got the distinct feeling that individuals expected me to show up and somehow we would "meet." It became necessary (in keeping with my own linear worldview and consequent assumptions of time and space) to approach individuals in person, introduce myself—stating where I came from ("who are your people?" was often first asked of me)—and then request an interview. When Salt River residents granted me interviews, I was immediately invited to their homes. Time, and to some extent space, seemed irrelevant when coordinating my research in the Salt River Community.

Communities must question their most basic cultural assumptions if they sincerely wish to challenge the dominant rationalized worldview. As David Harvey writes, "Any project to transform society must grasp the complex nettle of the transformation of spatial and temporal conceptions and practices" (1989:218). Without serious reflection on our most basic assumptions, our solutions merely become more of the same, though disguised in new forms. This is most clearly illustrated through the movement to develop "responsibly."

In place of sprawling master-planned communities, Cave Creek residents advocate for "responsible development," which is deemed less harmful to and in harmony with the environment. Responsibly developed homes typically use materials that help them blend into the natural landscape, minimize material consumption, and integrate many energy-saving devices. As Darcy, a Cave Creek resident, explains, responsibly developed homes "preserve the natural beauty of the desert."

However, the language of responsible development covers up the dramatic changes that occur when communities develop on the outskirts of major cities, whether responsibly or not. Between 1990 and 2000, Cave Creek grew by 27 percent. The Town of Cave Creek General Plan for 1993 projected a population of 8,600 people by the year 2010 (based on their plans for low-density development of one unit per 7.5 acres). Yet, in the General Plan adopted in March of 2000, the projected population for 2005 was already at 6,255 and the current population at 3,785. Given this rate of growth (65 percent in five years) the population in 2010 will be 10,321 people, far greater than the number projected in 1993 for 2010. Essentially, efforts to slow growth are adjusted as pressure to grow continues, yet the language of responsible development does not address the real growth that takes place and its potential repercussions to the town's visions of sustainability with its more fluid and symbolic orientation to nature.

It is also curious that in a survey of papers from January 1996 to December 1998 in both the *Arizona Republic* (Phoenix-based daily news) and the *Sonoran News* (weekly local paper for Cave Creek and the surrounding communities) and in all of my interviews with Cave Creek residents, the basic assumptions underlying responsible development remain uncritically accepted. Further analysis of *Arizona Republic* editorials from 2002 to

2003 reveals that growth is viewed as either a necessary good or a necessary evil, but definitely necessary and imminent. Responsible development is discussed frequently but rarely in depth. About half of the articles oppose further development without additional controls on development and half support growth. Discussion is centered not on whether growth should occur, or how to build in keeping with more traditional symbolic ideals, but on which plan is better. Those who advocate no development and no growth are so marginal and considered so radical that their voices are confined to a small peripheral audience.

Although responsibly developed homes employ green designs such as installing solar panels to save energy and harvesting rainwater, it is questionable whether the desert as an integral whole continues to exist as it did traditionally. Of course, this is partly due to zoning laws whereby even one home on every five acres may threaten the integrity of the desert as an ecosystem. However, the point is that responsible development has become the rationale through which we forget the larger question regarding how ecosystems function and what they can sustain.

Furthermore, low-density development generally gets equated with responsible development. Most of Cave Creek's residential areas are zoned for building one home on every five acres, although some areas have 2.5-acre zoning and other areas closer to town have one-acre zoning. Pavement or grass and foreign trees (such as palms) cover the desert floor in most areas of Phoenix, but residents of Cave Creek live among the cacti and native trees, bushes, sand, and rock, giving one the sense that residents seek to live with, and not overcome, the desert. Nevertheless, Cave Creek residents do not acknowledge the hidden costs of low-density development, which generally requires high-energy usage due to dependence on automobiles (for example, to travel into Phoenix for work), and low-density development supports construction of single-family homes with large indoor spaces that require extra cooling. Essentially, those who live in low-density areas tend to have larger "ecological footprints"[5] than the average urban dweller who lives in a smaller area, travels smaller distances, and tends to rely more on bikes and public transportation, thus consuming less energy. Cave Creek residents, though professing a more traditional view of nature, remain highly critical of urban dwelling while overlooking the potentially greater toll that their low-density living exacts upon the Earth. This is not to imply that urban dwelling is somehow more holistic. Those living in cities may have less of an individual impact on the land, but they still collectively support a rationalized orientation to land and development that encourages sprawl, not to mention whole-scale ecological destruction. For instance, Phoenix city residents have created so much pollution that a thick film of smog, popularly known as "the brown cloud," now continually hovers over the city.

Other social consequences also get overlooked in the pursuit of responsible development. Communities that advocate responsible development are generally affluent ones whose environmentalism seeks to preserve not simply the desert but the affluent lifestyle. In order to purchase a home tucked inconspicuously into the desert, a certain level of economic prosperity is necessary. Thus, responsible development often embraces the mainstream consumer values that it claims to challenge. The dirt-road foothills are accessible only by gas-inefficient SUVs, which epitomize the gluttony of overconsumption and add to the particulate pollution. Moreover, in their efforts to preserve a particular "lifestyle" such communities become segregated by economic, ethnic, and racial backgrounds. Ninety-five percent of Cave Creek residents are of Anglo-American descent with a median family income of $76,549 (U.S. Census Bureau 2000).

Places like Cave Creek, Arizona, stand as symbols of a larger cultural yearning to challenge the contemporary rationalist orientation. Residents who advocate and practice responsible development have their hearts in the right places. In American society, Cave Creek may be at the extreme end of environmental awareness and activism. However, the rules of the game are

These typical homes in Cave Creek, Arizona, serve as examples of "responsible development." Many homes in Cave Creek are built and designed in ways that avoid disturbing most of the native vegetation.

set by the dominant society and the culture in which we are raised. Anthropologist Edward Hall explained that "even when small fragments of culture are elevated to awareness, they are difficult to change, not only because they are so personally experienced but because people cannot act or interact at all in any meaningful way except through the medium of culture" (1966:188). Yet raising awareness seems crucial if we wish to begin to move beyond the rules of the dominant framework. If we choose to play by those rules, we are bound to find the playing field heavily tilted in favor of linear approaches to time and space that render land divisible and consumable.

I have learned that development forms in direct relation to our perceptions of time and space. The Pima elders' symbolic orientation to land traditionally encouraged development in direct relation to the immediate needs of the community. The land itself once offered basic sustenance to community members. Yet this

Taking a bird's-eye view of Cave Creek reveals that, although individuals may practice forms of responsible development, the land as a whole still gets developed. What kind of long-term strategies should communities consider when seeking to live sustainably?

was not some type of ideal world. The large exposed ditches used to irrigate, for example, led to rapid water evaporation. Nevertheless, the rational approach to land, while solving some problems, created others. The division of land into parcels, zoned for different uses, has rendered land a commodity. Developers seeking cheap land purchase it increasingly away from city centers, leading to leapfrog development. The large land areas necessary to develop master-planned communities promotes further sprawl. Even when communities like Cave Creek seek to develop "responsibly," basic rationalist assumptions about land continue to guide this growth.

I do not advocate a return to past models. Western societies also maintained a traditional orientation prior to the Age of Reason and the Scientific Revolution (Merchant 1980/1990:3). Renaissance imagery, Platonic and Neoplatonic symbolism, Aristotle, and Gnostic traditions all provide geocentric images of nature that locate human beings as part of nature, a nature perceived to be a living organism. Yet as Ken Wilber (1996) has pointed out, slavery and inequality (experienced by women, people of color, and lower socioeconomic classes) are often uncritically accepted in the same societies that do not perceive distinctions between the self and culture. At their extremes, both rational and traditional orientations can be dehumanizing. We tend to drift between extremes. In a highly rational society, without rejecting our orientations, we could think about how to integrate a symbolic and more fluid orientation more fully into our lives and into our culture today.

CHAPTER 3

SELLING "THE AMERICAN DREAM"

I first became interested in sprawl in the Southwest while reading through a pile of newspaper articles in my cramped Boston apartment. An article on Spur Cross Ranch caught my attention and I found myself intrigued by the mention of dream homes staged for development on acres and acres of some of the most exquisite land found in this country. Earlier I had been ruminating over my dream home in the New England countryside where I would lounge on my small garden terrace and drink tea while feeling embraced and protected by a dense pine forest. It became clear to me that these were two variations of the American Dream and that the American Dream is regionally influenced and nourished differently in different regions.

In contrast to my version of the American Dream, development in Spur Cross Ranch indicated a different dream—one where wide-open spaces and a type of frontier spirit guided development. The Southwestern Dream contains the American Dream of a private home, family, success and material wealth, with the added promise of wild experiences in the vast open frontier. After World War II, the Southwest, stimulated by successful defense spending contracts, growth of immigration and refugee populations, and movement of factory jobs into Sunbelt states, became a place where land, labor, and living costs were cheap. The cheap and abundant land of the Southwest was made habitable by the introduction of air conditioning, commercial airports, and government subsidies to develop dams and highways. Hence, the

Desert sprawl.

Southwest came to exemplify the American Dream—a place where every individual could make it in the land of plenty, owning land and a private home.

The individual may achieve the dream, but collectively we face a challenge. As Swaback described: "We have created an environment in which little differentiates one area from another. It is all a blur. Anything we cannot relate to we cannot love" (1997:38). Thus, although we may love our homes and even our planned communities, we despise the traffic congestion, health problems, overuse of limited water supplies, pollution, and smog that come along with sprawl. The suburb, a post-World War II rendition of the American Dream has, at its extreme, become an American nightmare.

The American Dream with a Southwest twist has been used to attract people into suburban areas and to legitimize the growth of these areas. The Dream has also inspired changes in the Salt River Community. A look at these changes provides further insight into how dominant idea systems have shaped our approaches to land. Ultimately, inspired by the American Dream, we have created a built environment that has led us to the point where our creations undermine our very dreams. Yet when we try to imagine different approaches to dwelling, we find that the Dream itself acts as a barrier to creating such change.

SELLING DREAMS

The promise of the American Dream is epitomized in the promotional literature of master-planned communities and major American cities. A look at this literature highlights the extent to which our commitment to the American Dream is exploited to drive and legitimize sprawl.

The American Dream is fueled by powerful conscious and subconscious forces, by drives that are often contradictory. To evoke complex emotions, master-planned community ads utilize "condensing symbols" (Turner 1974), broadly communicated words, phrases, or images that compact many widely shared ideas into one. A single ad may join multiple features of the American Dream, uniting ideas about community, individuality, family, recreation, affluence, middle-class values, youthfulness, and convenience, so as to equate living in a master-planned community with living the Dream. The American Dream in the desert also includes symbols about the frontier, freedom, and desert aesthetics. I have chosen a few ads from the March 17, 2001, "Home" section of the *Arizona Republic* to illustrate this, though we can take just about any master-planned community ad and uncover the way it uses various aspects of the American Dream to sell homes. Continued research through 2006 indicates no significant changes in the messages conveyed by such advertisements. Taken collectively, master-planned community ads read as an extended definition of the American Dream.

"If you are seeking a place where you and your family can live the active Arizona lifestyle without sacrificing your community—your search is over," states an ad for Power Ranch (*Ari-*

zona Republic, March 17, 2001:EV5). This ad draws on our nostalgia for the small-neighborhood feeling that we no longer experience in our sprawling communities. It maintains that the very design of the community will connect neighbors and also satisfy our recreational needs: "Power Ranch features its own parks, playgrounds, recreational amenities and the common thread of community that runs through everything the developers have done." The ad goes on to bridge our desires for community, aesthetics, recreation, education, consumption, and religion:

> Trails connect neighbor to neighbor and to the heart of the Community Park, lake and Clubhouse. A system of open spaces and parks offers a host of recreational opportunities to Power Ranch residents—all located near their home. Greenbelts and individual neighborhood landscaping design themes provide individual character. Proposed developments . . . include schools, shopping and a church—all right within the community.

The ad also promises that life in Power Ranch will meet the needs of growing families: "And as your family experiences those inevitable changes that occur over time—Power Ranch offers all that you will need." In this manner, we see how a single ad links various desires and conveys the message that the master-planned community will meet all of these desires.

A Johnson Ranch ad proclaims: "An area that is as rich in Western history as it is unpopulated. This is the best new place for living the rural Arizona life" (*Arizona Republic*, March 17, 2001:EV8). The irony, of course, is that the area has remained rural precisely because it is unpopulated, whereas master-planned communities can support tens of thousands of residents. The ad opens with an appeal to nostalgia for the rural West, but it goes on to describe how Johnson Ranch offers residents an array of modern conveniences: "Along with your home, you get the community recreation center including a park, playground, picnic pavilion, pool, spa and lighted basketball/tennis courts.

Some neighborhoods feature play parks. Your kids have their own K-5 school right within the community. You have ready access to two great 18-hole golf courses." Such advertising bridges the many contradictions inherent in the American Dream, linking seemingly opposite ideas like nostalgia for the past with visions of a modern future. Ultimately, advertisements claim that master-planned communities offer it all, including appeals to our middle-class sensibilities about optimizing our dollar. The ad concludes, "Obviously you get a big bang for your buck at Johnson Ranch. We planned it that way."

Master-planned community advertising also sells upward mobility. Fire Rock Country Club claims to offer "the ultimate gated private country-club lifestyle: 18 holes of golf that rank among the best in the Valley. An elegant clubhouse that'll take your breath away. Social and dining venues that elevate entertaining to an art. And of course, the beautiful, rolling Sonoran terrain" (*Arizona Republic*, March 17, 2001: EV11). Characterized as an amenity, the "rolling Sonoran terrain" is an apparent benefit to living the affluent lifestyle.

The same ad draws on Americans' sense of loss in a highly individualistic society. The Fire Rock Country Club proclaims: "Now that you've arrived you have somewhere you belong." Yet at the same time, the ad draws on the desire to express individuality, proclaiming, "Here is the custom home that you have always wanted." In customizing their homes, homeowners choose from a wide range of amenities suited to each individual's style. Paradoxically, if the ads are any indication, it seems that Americans desire to conform while asserting their individuality.

While selling "community," master-planned community advertising caters predominantly to American individualism. The ads insist that individual tastes drive people to purchase homes in the communities. Del Webb's Sun City, for example, claims itself "the life builder" and a place where you will "discover yourself" and follow your own unique taste. Del Webb advertises: "When people arrive at Sun City Grand, something amazing happens—they find themselves. Come find yourself at Sun City Grand." The ad emphasizes: "This is your time: Enjoy it your way" (Del Webb 2002). The master-planned community thus sells a privatized experience of community life. In essence, if we live in such a community, we will live in the best—"head and shoulders above everything else," claims Superstition Foothills—and, by association, we will *be* the best.

Promotional literature for cities around the country with populations of more than a million also use the American Dream to attract both visitors and new residents. Through an analysis of official city Web sites, we see that cities within various regions around the country sell different aspects of the American Dream. Northeastern cities recall their revolutionary history and how they plan to move into the future in interesting and exciting ways;[1] southern cities focus on excitement, celebration, and a future filled with possibilities;[2] midwestern cities tout the amenities of large metropolitan areas with a small-town feeling;[3] northwestern cities focus on their pragmatism;[4] and southwestern cities pride themselves as world-class "best" cities that offer a strong quality of life while continuing to grow.

In his State of the City address in 2005, Phoenix mayor Phil Gordon proclaimed that "this is the best available opportunity you're ever going to see in this Valley. Why here? Why now? Because this much room to grow, in the very heart of a major American city, is not available anyplace else." Over the past two decades, city leaders have consistently stressed that Phoenix is the best American city, filled with opportunity, and filled with open space for more opportunity. Mayor Gordon asks, "Can you imagine it? Can you see it? All that land. All that space. All those jobs. And all that opportunity. Phoenix is on the rise." He named Phoenix's enormous land base "Opportunity Corridor," stating, "There are more than 10,000 acres of opportunity there. Nearly 16 square miles." Hence land gets equated with opportunity, opportunity not merely for job growth, but opportunity for increased development.

In interviews with 167 migrants who moved from cities in the American Midwest or Northeast to cities in the Sunbelt, Hertz and colleagues (1990) observed that individuals follow their dreams west and south in a quest for "opportunity," and a "more open and flexible" social structure. Those who migrate to Sunbelt cities largely believe that they leave behind overcrowded troubled cities with decreased economic opportunities. The idea of "opportunity" takes on a very individualistic quality. Opportunity for community development, urban renewal, or environmental protection is secondary to opportunity for the individual. Hertz and colleagues concluded that "an individual ethic is substituted for a civic ethic. Self-interest replaces the public interest" (1990:263).

Discussions with Dana, a Cave Creek real estate agent, highlight the extent to which self-interest tends to overlook broader environmental problems like sprawl, which require collective community attention. Dana and I walk along the part of Cave Creek that runs through her backyard. She glances at the creek briefly and then, frowning, remarks that a land trust wants to purchase, and thereby protect, this section of Cave Creek. "I'm perfectly capable of maintaining it as well as they are. I don't build on it and nobody in their right mind would because the next flood would take it all out," Dana explains. "I don't believe you can tell me how to use my land because you like a desert view so I can't build a house here. And I'm just as capable as the next person of taking care of this creek."

Dana's position seems reasonable on a personal level, and it represents a position taken by many Americans, especially in regard to property rights (see Chapter 5). Yet this position equates freedom with strict individualism and what we lose in the process is the broader reality that individual choices are connected to the health and well-being of the community and environment. Although on an individual level we may care for our small piece of property, we have little ability individually to care for ecological systems that extend beyond property lines and across regions.

Del Webb advertisement featuring Peralta Trails at Superstition Mountains. The copy reads, "Sometimes It Takes A Mountain to Make You Feel Grounded. It is one thing to admire the Superstition Mountains from afar. To enjoy them from your own backyard can be a life-altering experience. Residents of Peralta Trails, a serene new community in Gold Canyon, paint vivid descriptions of the kinship they feel with the mountains and the strength they draw from living amid acres of unspoiled land. By offering fewer amenities in favor of more desert, Peralta Trails strikes the proper balance for people who don't need a lot to be happy. Only a lot of natural beauty."

Del Webb's Peralta Trails at Superstition Mountains. When one visits Peralta Trails, this is what one sees of this community with the Superstition Mountains in the residents' "own backyard."

Ultimately, the American Dream promises a life free from responsibility to the larger community. The Dream has evolved into what C. B. McPherson calls "possessive individualism," where individuals focus on their own economic interests. Sociologist Charles Derber (1996) has offered a bleak view of individualism in America today, warning that we live in a state of "individualism run amok" where the main thing that holds us together is no longer our families, schools, and other aspects of civil society, but rather our concern for the economy. Similarly, Bellah and colleagues (1985:271) maintain that "we have reached a kind of end of the line. The citizen has been swallowed up in 'economic man.'" We find ourselves propelled by self-interest, climbing the ladder of success where we must climb or be climbed upon. But where are we climbing?

THE AMERICAN DREAM
IN THE SALT RIVER COMMUNITY

It [the Southwest] is a dream. It is what people who have come
here from the beginning of time have dreamed. It's a dream landscape. To the Native American, it's full of sacred realities, powerful things. It's a landscape that has to be seen to be believed.
And as I say on occasion, it may have to be believed in order to
be seen. (Momaday 2005)

Scott Momaday's words echo a traditional native view of land:
land is sacred and intangible. As with traditional Pima views,
land is alive and mysterious, ungraspable, a living system that
must be honored. In contrast, pioneers who "settled" the West
carried with them a different dream of land characterized by
adventure, grit, and unyielding determination to expand and
realize their "manifest destiny."

It appears that the Salt River Community has managed to maintain open space, but the dominant culture's way of thinking about
land has permeated the community, challenging traditional
approaches to land. Tribal officials imagine a community that has
"the best of both worlds," as one leader told me. Business ventures
will bring prosperity and the promise of the American Dream to
the Pima people, while agriculture and the preservation of open
space will maintain traditional ideals. Many community members
do not believe the tribe has or will strike such a balance. They fore-
see a "checkerboard" reservation where the land becomes so fractionalized through leasing that one can no longer distinguish
between reservation and non-reservation land. Tribal officials
maintain that residents have a large say in the direction the tribe
moves, but many residents express a sense of disempowerment,
feeling that planning decisions have already been made regardless
of their opinions. And yet the American Dream—with its promises of a better life free from the daily economic struggle faced by
community members, 33.5 percent of whom fall below the

poverty level (U.S. Census 2000)—has had a great impact on the way community members think about and approach land.

The Pima Freeway has restructured land on the western border of the community, bringing with it economic prosperity for relocated families who sold their land to the Arizona Department of Transportation. The sudden prosperity attained through these land sales at first glance seems like the classic American story of the impoverished "making it" in the land of plenty. When driving around the reservation, it is easy to spot which homes belong to relocated families. They are affluent residences, often designed in a southwestern style with stucco walls and red tile roofing. Enclosed by high walls and elaborate security systems, these homes appear strangely out of place amidst the trailers and HUD (U.S. Department of Housing and Urban Development) housing in which many Pimas live. "You ever see the Barlay estate? These guys got the most out of the freeway," says Delbert, a Salt River Community member and psychologist. "When those Barlays walk anywhere, they're treated like Gods. Back in the '60s their houses were shacks; their houses were made out of tin and plywood."

Yet, for many, instant wealth and the achievement of the American Dream has turned into a nightmare as relocation and lack of knowledge about how to manage their wealth has had disturbing consequences. Many relocatees can no longer afford to maintain the opulent homes they purchased with the millions of dollars received from the land sales. From a distance these homes appear luxurious, but upon closer inspection we see that the wealthiest homes are in exceptionally poor condition. Furthermore, whereas prior to the land sales they had homes, even if only HUD homes, with relocation many eventually became homeless. Loreen explains, "Some still have money and they still have some of their land, but the money is gone now. And now their children are growing up and having families and they don't know where to put them."

"To move into a wealthy home, you think that would bring you happiness," says Lennard. "You know I could never put my finger on it until things started falling apart—my relationship, my work. The whole idea of relocating—because my wife said, 'I don't like coming home.' And I don't either. I do not like it. I guess we just never adjusted to being moved to a different place." Lennard maintains, "When you break up the nucleus of the family, something happens. Indian people, we start getting ill. We become sick. We're the type of people who don't just get up and go. I think that's what happens to Indian people."

The infusion of the American Dream over the past century into the Salt River Community has been a mixed blessing. Although the community has achieved greater economic gains, traditional ways of seeing and experiencing the land have given way to new ways of thinking about land, and with those changes have come changes to the way that development proceeds on the reservation. Change and cultural influence is in itself neither good nor bad. Cultures change and influence each other and we must take care not to associate Native American cultures with an idealized notion of an unchanging past. The Salt River Community must deal with the reality of changes to their community and collectively make important decisions that will affect how their community and land base develops for generations to come. Members of other reservations, as well as cities and towns throughout this country, face these same types of decisions. The decisions made now will influence who we become—whether we create thriving communities that sustain the health and well-being of both the people and the land or whether we continue on our current path and fulfill Swaback's bleak view of land conquered by sprawl, an "endless spread of unlovely, unlovable sameness" (1997:38).

RETHINKING BUILDING PATTERNS

Developers, planners, and city council members tell me that sprawl is a basic by-product of an expanding housing market. As discussed in Chapter 1, many planners believe that since sprawl will likely continue, it is important that we focus on *how* we develop this land. By this, planners often mean how best to design planned communities. Yet suburban sprawl is not necessary to expanding housing markets. Expansion of the housing market could include several other approaches, such as a continual recycling of the old into the new as in inner-city restoration projects, growing up and not out, or cluster development. Cluster development, for example, accommodates the same population size and even allows for population growth while also ensuring preservation of open space through placing homes closer together on smaller parcels of land. Land that would have been developed into individual lots is preserved as common open spaces. I find myself wondering why communities like Cave Creek, which certainly recognize the importance of open space, do not advocate more strongly for re-zoning efforts that would promote designs like cluster development.

One of the more obvious drawbacks to cluster development relates to zoning ordinances. As currently zoned, communities require conventional building patterns. The responsibility for changing these zoning requirements tends to fall on the developer, making the building process too time-consuming. Additionally, setting aside common open space in subdivisions requires homeowners' associations, which charge fees to maintain the open space. Furthermore, earlier models of such communities have not actually preserved much open space, which has soured many people on the idea of cluster development (Blaine and Shear 2005), although many rural towns have successfully incorporated open space features into the "traditional town" (Arendt 1994). Moreover, small lot sizes tend to be viewed unfavorably. The American Dream leaves little room for shared space; bigger is better and the individual should strive for private property.

Perhaps re-zoning for cluster development simply lies outside of conventional logic and is therefore overlooked as a viable option, as it requires large-scale community strategy in a society that magnifies the importance of the individual's wants and desires over that of the community's. To begin to be effective, cluster development requires large-scale regional planning. As David Quammen (1997) has reminded us, "ecosystem decay" in "a world that has been hacked to pieces" leads to habitat destruction and species extinction. Preserving small areas of land isolates species and leads to further extinction; thus the need for more broad-based regional planning. Yet, while some regional planning has taken seed in the United States, a far more comprehensive effort will need to take place; we really need to take seriously the importance of preserving yet larger areas of land so as not to create mere islands of preservation that end up isolating species. This will require greater public involvement in a time when Americans generally wish to remain socially and politically uninvolved[5] (Putnam 2000).

The increase in land trusts is a prospectively positive trend. In land trusts, groups purchase land for preservation or work out agreements to limit future development, thus protecting more than 800,000 acres of new land each year. Within only five years (1998–2003) the amount of acreage preserved through land trusts increased from 4.7 to 9.4 million (Land Trust Alliance 2006). Fifteen hundred private and nonprofit land trusts are currently working to conserve land around America at local and regional levels. In the Phoenix metropolitan area, nonprofit land trusts include the McDowell Sonoran Land Trust, the Desert Foothills Land Trust, and the Superstition Area Land Trust.

Although the growth in land trusts is promising and significant, it must be placed in the context of the rapid pace of development, which consumes more than two million acres of land per year. After he helped win a lawsuit to save Griggs Farm in Billerica, Massachusetts, conservationist Peter Forbes, with the Trust for Public Land (TPL), noted that

> we were victorious but at a huge cost. Late one night, I read our opponents annual report and learned that they had spent $587 million that same year buying other farms and forests for new development sites. This sum is equal to almost *half of all the*

money available at all levels of this nation's public and private sectors to conserve land. While we "won" in Billerica, a tidal wave of epic proportions had crashed over us, swept more places away, and we didn't even know it. (2001:38, Forbes's emphasis)

The drive to live the good life free of urban and suburban problems encourages development farther into the desert. Carrying dreams for a better life, we believe the good life is at the edge of the frontier and we often defy those who suggest that we consider and enforce restraint or consider these dreams in light of broader social and environmental concerns. When city officials place restrictions on development and water use in response to escalating populations that strain sparse supplies, they are often met with resistance. For instance, a Las Vegas Valley Water District investigator confronted a homeowner about his illegal sprinkler. "He got so angry," the investigator said, "he poked me in the chest and said, 'Man, with all these new rules, you people are trying to turn this place into a desert' " (Prugh 2000:90). Ultimately, what propels suburban sprawl is not only the drive to sell land and homes but also the drive to *consume* a certain form of growth.

CHAPTER 4

CONSUMING THE DREAM

While pursuing the American Dream, it seems that we have pushed out of reach the truly sustainable society, the society that "meets the needs of the present without compromising the ability of future generations to meet their own needs" (Brundtland Commission Report 1987). Many of us seek to escape from the problems of the growth society, migrating out of congested cities like New York and Los Angeles and now Phoenix, only to find ourselves recreating the problems we sought to escape. Perhaps we are drawn to sprawling communities because our hope, like a mirage, is ever settled on the horizon. As one Cave Creek resident said, "This place is already getting too crowded for me. I came here for the peace and quiet. Now I imagine I'll have to move another hundred miles into the desert to find any serenity."

New developments on the edges of crowded cities welcome those seeking refuge from the jostle and problems associated with urbanization. "Build it and they will come"—the maxim from the 1989 Universal Studios film, *Field of Dreams*—seems a fitting metaphor for these outlying developments. However, developers hold quite the opposite perception: the consumer wants it, so they will build it. As one developer states, "I think that most developers are geared toward what the buyer wants." Another explained that "development doesn't happen unless there's a need for it." Or in the words of a planner, "Ideally a lot of communities are planned based on the needs of the potential buyer. We generally have a good handle on what customers want through our company's extensive research needs analysis of the buyer."

Who is right? Which one came first: do consumer wants and needs drive development, or does development attract consumers? From a macro-sociological perspective, neither comes first; rather, both work in a dialectic, influencing each other, while at the same time a greater force drives both: a culture of consumption.

A culture of consumption shapes key ideas, values, and aspirations of the growth society. In a consumer society other social frameworks such as work, citizenship, or religion become secondary to the core social practice: consumption. Dreams themselves become something to purchase, not something to live or experience spontaneously. Consumption acts as a central organizing force, central to how individuals negotiate identity and social status and central to how they orient their daily activities. In the consumer society consumption also spills into other social practices. For example, as noted in Chapter 1, although the planning industry originally promoted a strong social reform agenda, a market-driven model now largely directs the industry. Yet in a "positive" way, individuals living in a consumer society are formally "free," and choices remain unbound by legally determined social roles.

In a consumer society, any social phenomenon can, in theory, become a commodity. Sustainability itself has become a product of the market, for values such as "simple living" are good business. A search on Amazon.com in July of 2007 resulted in 10,486 books on "simple living." Type "simple living" into a Google search and you come up with 1,300,000 hits. Magazines like *Real Simple* sell the "simple life." Ironically, 48 percent of the May 2005 issue is sponsored by the mainstream advertising industry touting products from Ralph Lauren, Lancôme, Gap Kids, Mabelline, and Mercedes-Benz—not strong promoters of the simple life. A lavatory faucet featured on the cover sells for $1,440 and the console sells for $2,250.

This appears to be the culture of consumer leisure, not simplicity and sustainability.

THE FREEDOM TO CONSUME

Migration to the West has persisted unabated through the twentieth and into the twenty-first century. The last U.S. Census identified western states as the fastest growing states in the nation. Maricopa County, Arizona, experienced the third highest rate of net domestic in-migration in the country with an average of 42,066 new residents per year between 2000 and 2004 (U.S. Census Bureau 2006). A small number of residents, mostly of retirement age, leave Phoenix and Maricopa County to move to cooler climates, and a growing number of Phoenix area workers leave and commute from more distant towns like Casa Grande, Arizona (W. P. Carey School of Business 2001). Still, between 1990 and 2000, the population in the Phoenix metropolitan area increased by 40 percent, with equally dramatic increases in other desert cities[1] (U.S. Census Bureau News 2005). Between 2000 and 2004, the Phoenix-Mesa-Scottsdale region has seen average annual population increases of 13.9 percent (Perry 2006).

The desert continues to summon the American frontier spirit, calling Americans to migrate to Sunbelt cities in search of the "endless dream." As Hertz and colleagues have written, "The frontier may be closed but the idea that it represents in the American psyche remains alive: when things get bad you can always move on" (1990:268). Consequently, movement west has long been associated with freedom and an extension of the American Dream. The wide-open spaces of the western states would "long retain their primeval simplicity of manners and incorruptible love of liberty," said George Washington (1789) in his first inaugural address. Henry David Thoreau reinforced this equation of the West with freedom when he wrote, "Eastward I go by force; but westward I go free" (1854/1973:86). Ironically, the "West" continues to be associated with movement and freedom despite the fact that many new residents now move east to Arizona from California (U.S. Census Bureau News 2003).

The consumer culture of the past half-century has also embraced this romanticized message and, as with the "simple life," has turned "freedom" and the pioneer spirit of the Old West into marketable commodities. "Freedom" is incorporated into the names of businesses all around Phoenix. "Freedom Wireless," "Freedom Mortgage," "Freedom Manor," "Freedom Auto Works," "Financial Freedom," and "Club Freedom" are just a few of the businesses that use the idea of "freedom" to market products.

I walk around downtown Cave Creek and feel as though I am walking through an embellished advertisement of the Pioneer West. Stereotypical western paraphernalia such as saddles, ropes, old western pictures, and western boots decorate dark walls of restaurants and bars. A shopping area called "Frontier Town" sells t-shirts painted with images of cowboys and old gold mines. Signs for "Buffalo Chip Saloon," "Horny Toad Restaurant," "The Satisfied Frog," and "Tumbleweed Hotel" tell us where the West has gone: into our restaurants, hotels, and shops. I walk under a white stucco archway into a Mexican restaurant for lunch, and I'm suddenly gazing upon a tropical paradise. No sign of the desert in here. Palms and other tropical shade trees line a pond where ducks leisurely swim around and bathe themselves under the cool waterfall trickling down the side of a rock-fall. I temporarily forget that the dry desert lies just outside of this idyllic setting, until a wave of heat reminds me of my whereabouts. Yet as I am quenched by a mango ice tea while sitting alongside the pond, the desert disappears. I too consume the dream and temporarily enjoy the manufactured environment designed to make consumption easy.

Ultimately, the freedom of the West gets equated with a consumer-oriented freedom. The freedom to consume discourages any suggestion that we limit where we live and consider how we build. Many view increased local, state, or federal regulations

Downtown Cave Creek. Shop facades exhibit stereotypes of the Pioneer West.

as infringements on individual rights and contrary to the American Dream. Ron, a developer and resident of Cave Creek, maintains that while he may not like how his neighbors build their homes or block his views, it is their "free choice" to build as they wish. "If I own a piece of desert, I can do anything I want with it," maintains Ron. "I can put a junk yard there. I can put a cemetery there. Of course, I still have a responsibility to be a good neighbor, and I am. But this is my free choice, not the government's choice."

"Freedom of choice" guides not only discussion about building practices but also discussion about homeownership. Developers and consumers alike contend that homebuyers' "individual tastes" guide the development of new homes in master-planned communities on the edges of desert cities. Through "customizing" their homes, homebuyers may choose among three types of tiles, four types of countertops, and five types of cabinet fixtures. Furthermore, residents are privy to countless amenities designed to satisfy their every desire. From fitness clubs to game rooms to

The Freedom to Consume. This is an image of a Mexican restaurant in Cave Creek, Arizona, where I leisurely sipped mango iced tea in a "tropical paradise," forgetting that the Sonoran Desert lay just meters away.

team sports, life in the desert offers an endless stream of choices designed to suit the individual. "We believe in these communities, which are highly amenitized," one Del Webb planner explained. "That means they have golf courses, recreation centers, computer labs, theater groups, et cetera."

While catering to consumer choice, planned communities regulate, among other things, what homeowners can plant, the colors they can paint their homes, and how many visitor cars can park on driveways. Surveillance cameras to protect residents from possible intruders can be found anywhere, from pool decks to elevators to hallways. In the Southwest, where the myth of the rugged individualist free from social constraints continues to thrive and guides a type of unfettered development, such regulations seem to insulate and guide our dreams. Nevertheless, residents find in master-planned communities ready-made neighborhoods that make it easy to experience many other valued ways of living. They don't have to do the work of creating a community with recreational and educational opportunities for the children or seek out new friends, community events, and so on. Rather, the master-planned community creates these opportunities and offers a pre-packaged lifestyle where "minor sacrifices," as one resident put it, seem small prices to pay for the luxuries gained. Essentially, the freedom to consume guides individuals farther into the desert, even while other freedoms recede.

Consuming the "Desert Lifestyle"

Communities growing along the outer edges of southwestern cities do not merely sell freedom, they market a "desert lifestyle," which regards the desert itself as an amenity. The emphasis is mine in the following examples: "Experience an *exclusive desert lifestyle* in the golf course community of DC Ranch" (DC Ranch 2006). "In the heart of vibrant north Scottsdale, Arizona, Silverleaf offers an artful design for *desert living*"

(DMB Associates 2006). "From our *desert resort* condominiums and golf casitas to our mountain retreat cabins and homes, Mirage Homes can help you 'resort to a better lifestyle' today!" (Mirage Homes 2006).

The language of desert living is not limited to advertisements. The term "desert lifestyle" is one of the most common catchphrases (as common as "sustainability" and "responsible development") used by Phoenix area residents to describe the lifestyle they enjoy. However, I have never come across a single Salt River Pima–Maricopa Indian Community member who used this term. This indicates how specific the idea is to a particular cultural group and to a particular approach to living.

The "desert lifestyle" goes further than simply turning the desert into an amenity, for the phrase defines a whole new way of living in the desert. Once thought of as barren and incapable of sustaining life, today the desert is central to the resort-style living that distinguishes life in the Valley of the Sun. Residents equate living in the desert with its more than three hundred days of sunshine each year, with living in a tropical paradise minus the excessive rainfall of the tropics. Yet, ironically, the "desert lifestyle" includes abundant quantities of water. From one of the world's largest fountains, surging 560 feet into the air at Fountain Hills, to man-made lakes flowing around master-planned communities and golf courses, to elaborate pools with waterfalls and tropical trees surrounding opulent resorts and industrial parks, water is an integral part of the Phoenix metropolitan landscape and a key feature of the desert lifestyle.

Catalina Bay, a community situated near a man-made lake in Gilbert, Arizona, just east of Phoenix, illustrates the desert lifestyle. My visit to Catalina Bay transported me to a tropical paradise where large flowering trees loom over the entrance and whose name maintains the illusion of the desert as oasis. Once in Catalina Bay, I am invited to suspend my understanding that this really is a desert. I have entered a fantasyland. I am invited to not simply enter the fantasy, enjoy it and leave it, but to *believe*

Consuming the "desert lifestyle." Immense quantities of water flow in all parts of this desert city. Water flows in front of banks, in human-made lakes, and as waterfalls in front of businesses, as in the image shown here.

it. *This is the desert.* Luxury homes adorn the water's edge, as do motorboats, fish, ducks, and hundreds of palm trees. I feel as though I have been transported to a coastal community amidst the cool water of a meandering bay. I look more carefully and discover that the water is an iridescent green color, but I will not look *too* closely lest I break my subconscious agreement to suspend reality. Gazing across the bay, I view a couple wearing blue canvas boat shoes, walking to their motorboat. After all, they need not worry about those prickly cacti ready to stick them when traipsing through the desert brush. There is no desert brush. Black paved streets, four-square-foot front lawns, four-thousand-square-foot homes, and a lush waterway constitute the land here.

The "desert lifestyle" may be thought of as a self-enclosed system in which individuals engage in what Baudrillard (1970) called a game of signification. In his analysis of consumer society, Baudrillard identified "networks of signifiers" whereby the consumer relates not merely to the object but to the symbolic meaning beneath the object. Thus, when purchasing a home in a planned desert community, we do not merely purchase a home, we purchase an entire network of meaning, a lifestyle and all that lifestyle promises. The couple walking out to their motorboat seems to perfectly embody this. They play the rules of the game so well that they appear to believe that the simulation of California's Catalina Bay in the middle of the Sonoran Desert *is* reality.

Through careful manipulation of the environment, a tropical paradise replaces a desert that receives only seven inches of rainfall per year. In order to simulate this tropical paradise, millions of acre-feet of ground water are pumped out from beneath the desert floor. Each of the Phoenix area's 189 golf courses (Golfable.com 2005) consumes an average of 2.3 million acre-feet of water per year (Golf Industry Association 2003). Yet developers and planners consistently maintain that much of the water for golf courses comes in the form of effluent, otherwise

Phoenix golf courses. The Phoenix area has 189 golf courses, each of which consumes an average of 2.3 million acre-feet of water per year.

known as gray water or treated waste water. Nevertheless, effluent depends on constructing enough homes with enough residents to produce the effluent. Golf courses have become the primary amenity sought by more prosperous residents. Dan, a journalist in Cave Creek, assured me that the only way Spur Cross Ranch would get developed was if a golf course was authorized: "The winning developments, the ones who have made a lot of money, are the ones who have golf courses."

There is a general resistance to thinking about why we are drawn to such communities and a willingness to blind ourselves to the ecological destruction in which we engage. We do things like casually walk out in our boat shoes to our human-constructed bays, all the while pretending that pumping up ground water to flood the desert has no effect. Yet all with whom I spoke, whether living in a master-planned community, low-density housing development, or on reservations, and whether community members, planners, developers, or politicians, tell me that they value ecological sustainability. Even developers, often demonized by those fighting sprawl, value sustainability. Ron argued that developers are some of the more ecologically sensitive individuals involved in shaping development in the desert. "Contrary to popular opinion, I am probably a better environmentalist than people running around loose on this planet denying others the right to use their property in the ways they see fit. The real problem is we have more people on this planet than we ever had."

One of the most widespread arguments used against rethinking the growth society and the consumer culture that fuels it is that somehow this society must meet the needs of a growing population. This argument continues in politics, the media, and mainstream social discourse: people have nowhere else to go, nowhere as affordable, nowhere as safe, and nowhere with such a range of amenities. This is the good life. After all, don't we have the right to improve our social conditions? Should we not seek out the American Dream with all of its promise and hope? Perhaps, but let us not forget that we are here for the Dream, not because there was no room for us elsewhere. We are in the habit of blaming population growth, immigration, and poor living conditions for our growing suburbs. Yet, the poor continue to occupy the inner city and immigrants continue to make the inner city thrive.[2] Ultimately, our sprawling suburbs maintain a distinctly affluent character. As Jeff Gersh has highlighted, sprawling new developments are demographically different from traditional rural communities because they consist of retirees receiving benefits, entrepreneurs, and "baby boomers currently on the receiving end of an enormous intergenerational transfer of wealth" (Gersh 1996:17). "The trouble is," according to Gersh, that "only the wealthy can live in such places. As housing prices rise, firemen, housekeepers, and other members of the non-leisure class are obliged to live elsewhere and commute to work." Hence, additional bedroom communities composed of those who service the affluent communities define a second category of sprawl.

The desert lifestyle sounds attractive until we really begin to examine its implications. Certainly, it is easier and nicer to live within our mythologies and to continue to build on the storyline of life in the Wild West with its rugged individualism and promises of freedom and the good life. In the words of historian Bernard De Voto: "The loveliest myth of all America was the far West . . . a lost, impossible province where men were not dwarfs and adventure truly was."

Consuming the Myth

Bernardo De Voto's image of the American West contrasts with today's Wild West, which comes prepackaged for consumption. We may purchase "custom outdoor adventures" that, as with Southern Arizona Adventures (2006), feature a "fun, safe, interactive, journey into the ancient Old West." We may even consume the Grand Canyon, the quintessential icon of the great American West. Ironically, there is an IMAX theater just a mile from the South Rim of the Grand Canyon that features *Grand Canyon: The Hidden Secrets*. Playing to more than thirty-five million viewers over the past twenty years, the film is currently known as "the top-grossing IMAX® film of all time" and the theater is "Arizona's Top Tourist Attraction" (Destination Cinema 2004). The Grand Canyon Imax Theater maintains that watching the film is "the only way you can, in 35 minutes, get an overview of the spectacular vistas, the history of its explorations, and the hidden canyon experiences not available on any tour." In America, natural beauty is a commodity to be packaged, sold, and experienced as a virtual reality.

Many migrating to or visiting the Southwest consume a myth, not only of the Old West but of consumption itself. As Baudrillard (1970) noted, the consumer society thrives because collectively the society has developed and consumed the myth of consumption. This myth has become a type of "social cement" (Marcuse 1964) that replaces the other social bonds like family and community that once connected individuals to each other and to their environment. In essence, just as we consume televised images (of, for example, perfect bodies, happy families) that are mere shadows of ourselves fed back to ourselves for us to emulate, likewise we consume a lifestyle that advertises itself to us in simplified form. We consume the activity of consumption. We purchase the advertised home in the desert as a way of satisfying some need as if this vaunted caricature of life, with its neon painted pools and its Disney-like recreational facilities (Anthem even has a children's train-ride encircling its gardens) could satisfy real human needs.

We do not merely consume an idea or acquire a false need in Marxian terms. We are more than collectively fooled into believing that we need something that we do not really need, thus developing a false consciousness. The process is far more insidious than that. We are not mere pawns of dominant groups like the housing industry or of developers who somehow brainwash consumers into believing this lifestyle will satisfy our needs; we live in an age where consumption is an end in itself and is the ultimate road to happiness. As John Updike (1979) once said, "America is a vast conspiracy to make you happy."

Aldous Huxley (1932) predicted the controlling effects that our obsessions with happiness and pleasure would have in *Brave New World* where individuals are controlled by what Baudrillard has called "joyful conformity," a dutiful obligation to experience pleasure. Partaking in the enjoyment of pleasure becomes not only the means through which we garner value and truth but also a duty to which we must joyfully conform lest anyone imagine something wrong with us. We must be happy and we continually wonder what is wrong with us when we do not feel happy.

The desert lifestyle markets a type of perfected existence where the sun always shines (literally and figuratively) and no other emotion but pure bliss seems even possible. The institutionalization of pleasure goes beyond mere plans to build communities around endless amenities. Ultimately, everything is

The water from the Salt River has been diverted through canals to feed the Phoenix metropolitan area; however, the bottom of the original Salt River bed is mined for gravel and silt. Some of this is used by the Phoenix Cement Company, a Salt River Community enterprise.

viewed with reference to its capacity to offer pleasure—even the desert itself. One developer describes the consumer vision of the desert quite eloquently:

> What makes the Phoenix metropolitan area the desert is definitely the fact that we still have a footprint of a desert in the city and you can literally live and work and play within this kind of urban desert environment. I think that is great. I climb Squaw Peak all the time. I live not too far and I can get up here.

Thus, we still have a "footprint of a desert in the city": the Phoenix metropolitan area *is* the desert according to this developer. We can consume *and* preserve as long as the footprint still exists. When nature is rearranged for our "pleasure," what is lost?

Developers, planners, and consumers alike are caught up in a web of significance (as are people of all cultures) that makes the golf courses, security systems, clubhouses, water parks, ballparks, and desert view all appear to be necessary. These amenities are justified from the developer's viewpoint because consumers appear to indicate through buying patterns that they want highly amenitized communities. Likewise, consumers seek to maximize their dollar and experience their birthright: the American Dream.

Human cultures have generated unlimited housing styles from hogans to pueblos to apartment buildings to master-planned communities, but building in the desert, whether characterized as "responsible" and planned or "irresponsible" and haphazard, takes on a distinctly cultural dimension guided by our consumer values. "Should we all live in pueblos then?" calls out the brave student from the back of one of my classes. Pueblos work for particular cultural groups, but the point is not that we must choose another cultural formula, but rather that we must earnestly question our own living arrangements.

CHAPTER 5

RIGHTS WARS
AND DEVELOPING
A LAND ETHIC

We must ask ourselves some basic questions: What is land? What has land come to mean to us as a culture? The march of sprawl indicates a vision of the land as a sea of dead matter, but a growing part of the culture recognizes that *land is life*. Peter Forbes wrote poetically that "land is the sweep of one's heart, and the place where we play out our greatest struggles. . . . This morning there is a woman in my view of this open pasture. She stands alone with acres and acres of grass around her. Her hands are in her pockets and her legs are soaked with dew as she faces east to be warmed by the early morning sun. *Land is love*" (2001:2, Forbes's emphasis).

Yet we have few avenues through which to express love and care for the land. Values around land preservation largely get played out in the court system and through the legislative process. Although legislation often acts to institutionalize a particular set of values (for example, the Civil Rights Act of 1964 institutional-ized racial equality), I maintain that transforming the ways in which we think about land and community is crucial to shifting our approaches to living on the land. Living in the Southwest for the past ten years has brought about a personal shift. I realize that land has value in itself and has its own power. I realize that land wars ignore the third, middle party: the land. In this way, I feel like an unofficial ambassador between warring factions.

I have become aware of how the focus on legal victories alone acts to distract us from the reflection and community building that must go on within and outside of the litigation process. In the macro-picture, small victories may be possible, but such legal battles have not and likely will not slow down suburban growth.

RIGHTS WARS

Land rights battles are about power and about whose positions get heard. They are also about how our constructed meanings of land find voice in two mutually exclusive positions and how we take sides in order to assure that our vision of reality becomes *the* vision of reality. Those on either side of the battle line claim that they cannot understand the other's position and that ultimately it is invalid and even evil. The liberal advocates of the preservation of nature and the conservative advocates of property rights appear as hostile and antagonistic as any other opponents in human history.

The fundamental right to property has a secure place in American history and in our Constitution. The Fifth Amendment states among other things that "No person shall. . . be deprived of life, liberty, or property, without due process of law; nor shall private property be taken for public use, without just compensation." The Fourteenth Amendment reasserts the states' responsibilities to uphold due process.[1] We understand that without these rights, tyranny may find fertile ground. Property rights advocates view environmental regulations as imminent threats to such rights. Nancie G. Marzulla, former president and founder of Defenders of Property Rights, has written that "the goal is to reclaim basic constitutional rights to own and use property in a responsible and safe manner, safe from the suffocating web of environmental regulations that now touch every form of property use and ownership" (1995:1).

Environmentalists, on the other hand, focus on environmental preservation legislation, arguing that our constitutional rights do not give us the right to destroy ecologies. The debate between

Rights poster. This poster stood at the entranceway to Spur Cross Ranch.

property rights and environmental preservation engenders difficult questions. For example, which has greater priority: the right
of the spotted owl to exist or the right of the lumber industry and
its employees to their livelihood? In the case of Cave Creek, the
battle lines got drawn around Spur Cross Ranch. Here the rights
of riparian areas and indigenous archeological sites were set
against the right of the owners to develop their land and build a
master-planned community. Each side labels the other side as
evil and proceeds to demonize the other in an attempt to delegit-
imize its position.

Environmentalists called those who supported development
of Spur Cross Ranch "monsters," "dragons who always rear their
ugly heads," "needless destroyers," and "way out of control."
Likewise, developers and property rights advocates accused
environmentalists of "restricting freedom," acting as a "police
power," "preserving at the expense of people," "abusing land
owners," "denying people their property rights," and being
"NIMBYists (Not in My Backyard)." The battles get quite ugly
as each group views its rights as fundamental. The reality is that

both views are correct. In our legal system, however, only one view can "win" and thus rights arguments tend to lead groups and individuals into some of the most heated dramas of our day. Protection of land has consistently been framed as a legal issue. Amy Silverman (1999), journalist for the *Phoenix New Times*, has articulated a broadly held position: "condemn the land." She argued that politicians made "a good faith effort to save Spur Cross, doing just about everything in their power to make things right with the property owners." "To heck with it," Silverman concluded. "Condemn the land. See ya in court."

Likewise, those who take a property rights perspective also view land in legal terms. Dana, the Cave Creek real estate agent introduced earlier, maintains that the right to develop property supercedes environmental problems that may come with that development. "It's a matter of my legal rights as an American citizen," explains Dana. "Each little freedom that we give away for a 'common good' is one more gone that never comes back. Individual freedom is an important thing. Freedom of speech is an important thing. And private property rights, the right to use, own and transfer your property, are equally as fundamental."

Property rights advocates consistently accuse environmentalists of trying to impose government restrictions on individuals, and environmentalists accuse property rights advocates of only caring about the bottom line while overlooking ecological issues. Our society is organized to play out this and any drama that takes polar opposite positions in the court system.

Throughout the country we find ourselves swinging on a political and legislative pendulum. The federal and state courts have no fixed approach to settling property rights disputes and constitutional interpretations are shaped by the socio-political-economic context in which they are made. Hence, the New Deal era, in response to the 1930s Great Depression, called for greater government intervention, diminished the focus on a laissez faire uncontrolled free market philosophy, and ushered in the regulatory state that viewed property rights issues as secondary to civil rights issues. However, the 1990s brought shifts in the political and intellectual climate, guiding consequent shifts in approaches to property rights. This was precipitated in the 1970s and in the 1980s, particularly with President Reagan's judicial appointees, who were more supportive of property rights perspectives. While the courts took a markedly conservative shift (Sontag 2003), environmentalists won their own series of legal battles in the 1990s that resulted in, for example, the Oil Pollution Act of 1990 (OPA), the Pollution Prevention Act (PPA) in 1990, the Food Quality Protection Act (FQPA) in 1996, and the Chemical Safety Information, Site Security and Fuels Regulatory Relief Act in 1999. Land battles unfold in the courts and through the legislative process and meanwhile sprawl marches on because we focus as a society on legislating without attending to and understanding the meaning behind the battles.

In a society that honors a "winner takes all" approach, the winners of lawsuits are validated and the losers are subdued. But this overlooks the care that lies beneath many groups' claims. Whether environmentalists, planners, developers, or politicians, Cave Creek residents describing Spur Cross Ranch often mentioned its exquisite beauty. Yet discussion inevitably returned to the legal ramifications surrounding the dispute. Somehow we do not think that our feelings for the land can or should stand on their own; our feelings for nature must be couched in the language of politics or legislation. Although the battle got settled out of court, reducing Spur Cross Ranch to a legal matter often overlooked the deeper meaning of this land for community members.

The defensive nature of litigation distracts us from these deeper truths. As noted by Dana (see Chapter 3), property rights advocates may care about land just as much as environmentalists. Environmental historian William Cronon observed that even those who build on the fragile land of mountainsides do so not because they want to destroy land or place their families and themselves at any risk but because they want to be close to nature's beauty (1995:32). Litigating against individuals or groups to force collective care of land not only overlooks the reality that many do feel for the land but also sets the stage for legitimizing our dehumanization of each other: litigation places us in the role of defining the other as enemy.

Land does get preserved through rights claims; however, legislation to preserve land draws on legislation for *other* rights, not the mere rights of land or nature. Land gets preserved through application of the Endangered Species Act of 1973 or the Archaeological Resources Protection Act of 1979. However, we do not feel justified in our efforts to preserve land merely because we care about land. A woman from the Nature Conservancy was asked to speak to the people of a town near Penobscot Bay, Maine, about what she found "important" about their land. As noted by Forbes, "She came to realize, by their choice of the word *important*, that the townspeople wanted her to find land with rare and endangered species, land *worthy* of protection. But she also knew from her visit that what the people of this town really *loved* were the blueberry barrens. . . . Those blueberry barrens enabled those people to be *of that place*." Forbes asks, "Why is it, then, that they needed someone else to tell them that they could protect what they loved? Why is it that they needed the excuse of being home to endangered species to protect it?" (2001:29, Forbes's emphasis).

When individuals unite to preserve land because they feel responsible for that land, because they cannot bear to see that land transformed into housing units or industrial parks, legislation is often the route through which they express themselves. In American society the legislative process is the only process powerful enough to represent care of land. But can the litigious society with its documents and policies effectively legislate care and stewardship of the land? What else is needed to stop sprawl?

COMMUNITY BUILDING AND A LAND ETHIC

To curb sprawl we need to transform our relationships with the land. Sprawl results from an excessively narrow view of land: as a resource to be used. Yet, as noted by Forbes, "the long-term cure for the loss of wilderness is not merely buying and protecting some wildlands but rebuilding a culture of sympathy for and reliance on the land, just as the complete prevention of another heart attack isn't bypass surgery but changing the patient's way of life. . . . The ecological solution is to rethink land conservation as the conservation of culture" (2001:39). The focus on conserving culture and building community seems necessary if we wish to approach the problem of sprawl through positive, life-affirming means, rather than through contentious and often mean-spirited lawsuits that characterize our current approaches to land preservation.

A community is commonly described as a group of people residing in a certain location. However, recognizing community in broader terms is critical if we wish to rebuild a culture of sympathy and form connections with the land that move us away from objectifying and ultimately destroying it. Community derives from the Latin *munus*, meaning "gift," and *cum*, meaning "together." Community thus means "giving together." Our community is a boundless support system, embracing us and giving to us in all that we do.

Our first and deepest sense of community occurs within the family. But we soon recognize the greater supporting frameworks that assist us all throughout our lives. If we look carefully enough at the world around us, we discover that this supporting community encompasses, quite literally, everything. My very ability to type this sentence, for example, is assisted by a limitless community. One can only imagine the network of individuals and machines used to build and operate the hydroelectric dams that produce the energy that enables me to type this sentence into my computer. What type of resources went into producing the PowerBook G4 Apple computer that remembers and recalls this entire manuscript every time I seek to add to it? My body is fueled this morning with a wheat tortilla, cheese, and grapes. Scores of individuals worked to transform the milk to cheese and the wheat to tortilla. I imagine all of the individuals involved in picking grapes and the huge industries developed in order to enable these products to travel around the country and often the world in order to make it to my kitchen table. Furthermore, my computer sits upon a pine wood table. What labor went into its production and how many trees were sacrificed in order that I may have something upon which to type? Of course, there is the land I live on and the shelter that protects me. In order to write these words, I must rely on an immeasurably large community, one that ultimately encompasses the entire world. Through understanding the living and non-living world that sustains us, even at the level of mundane activities like completing this sentence, through comprehending the vast networks that nurture us as children and nourish us throughout our lives, our sense of community grows. From here it is a short step to relate to, and experience reverence, respect, and care for all that surrounds us, for all that we call *nature*.

Through developing a broader sense of community and reestablishing relationships with the land, we can move beyond litigation, which is currently the main way that individuals and groups feel they can "save" the land quickly enough. In a litigious climate, we cannot do what we really need to do amongst ourselves and within our communities: develop a land ethic.

With its introduction in 1949, Aldo Leopold's "land ethic" shaped modern forest management practices and also influenced the 1970s environmental movement and today's calls for sustainability and responsibility. A land ethic extends our ideas of community. In his classic, *A Sand County Almanac*, Leopold wrote, "The land ethic simply enlarges the boundaries of the community to include soils, waters, plants, and animals, or collectively: the land" (1949:239). The land ethic recognizes that human beings are part of the ecology of an area, not masters of it.

Leopold maintained that "the evolution of a land ethic is an intellectual as well as an emotional process" (1949:263) and encouraged us to consider land itself in moral terms. He challenged us to extend moral consideration beyond a sense that only human beings are capable of reason and feeling or have an interest in what becomes of this land. Whereas Western philosophy traditionally distinguishes between nature and culture, Leopold did not perceive such a divide. He asserted that humans are "ecological selves"—intimately connected with and part of "nature." Thus, Leopold was the first Western intellectual to maintain that ecosystem integrity, diversity, and beauty are morally relevant human values. He redefined what it means to be human, suggesting that—in contrast to the Cartesian model of "I think, therefore I am"—emotion, care, love, and empathy make us human. Therefore, Leopold called on all individuals to rethink their relationships with the land and the greater biotic community.

RESPONSIBILITIES AND THE LAND ETHIC

"An ethic, ecologically, is a limitation on freedom of action in the struggle for existence" (238), wrote Leopold. Thus, developing a land ethic means *choosing* to limit ourselves. Rights indicate that to which we are privileged, while ethics awaken our responsibilities—responsibilities to the land and to one another. Leopold wrote that "all ethics so far evolved rest upon a single premise: that the individual is a member of a community of interdependent parts. His instincts prompt him to compete for his place in the community, but his ethics prompt him also to co-operate" (239).

Continuing to develop a sense of responsibility for the land is the only lasting way of preserving land from sprawl. Preservation often comes about because it has been legislated, but I suggest that preservation born out of anything but our collective sense of care and responsibility is subject to rapid deterioration. It would be much more difficult to pave over land if we *felt* for land and the life that land supports. What would our approaches to property rights and environmentalism look like if imbued with a land ethic?

Property rights advocates care and work to preserve their individual property; however, a land ethic requires us to extend our sense of responsibility beyond individual property borders. Theoretically, we may understand that our freedom is always subject to our responsibility to others. We do not have the freedom to do anything we want with our land, if what we want places others at risk. Yet while we understand that we must limit our freedom of action in response to other human beings, we have not extended this understanding to the land or to nature.

Extending our sense of community beyond the human community and into the community of all beings that support and sustain us challenges our sense of property rights—requiring us to extend these rights not only to the individual's right to own property but to nature's right to thrive. Yet, recognizing the rights of nature, or the rights of any group, requires those in power to relinquish resources. Whereas slavery was once viewed as "free labor," subject to certain laws and management styles, "nature" is viewed today as a free resource to be appropriately managed. To recognize the rights of nature brings with it a set of responsibilities and a loss of what has been viewed as "free resources." It brings the very notion of "resources" into question because recognition of nature's rights implies that nature has intrinsic value not subject to human use. In other words, true recognition of the rights of nature would require a restructuring of the entire economy.[2]

Through extending our sense of responsibility beyond individuals and into the greater community, it becomes impossible to view our livelihoods as distinct from the livelihoods of everything that lives around us and sustains us. It becomes our responsibility not only to protect the rights of the individual but also to work collectively to ensure that how we live does not harm the larger Earth community.

Some environmental activism is imbued with a land ethic; however, much anti-sprawl activity supports policies that also maintain limited views of land and community. For example, the practice of transferring development rights from more aesthetically pleasing lands to less aesthetically pleasing lands—what I call "environmental triage"[3]—also sustains growth. Through environmental triage, "less" desirable land may be sacrificed to preserve "more" desirable land. At one point a land swap was promoted as a means to preserve Spur Cross Ranch. While opposing development in Spur Cross Ranch, many agreed to development in an area of undeveloped "empty" desert in North Scottsdale as part of a land swap. Although the swap became mired in controversy and the state ultimately agreed to designate Spur Cross Ranch as a preserve without a land swap, the support of development on another part of the desert indicates a specifically narrow notion of preservation. This activity maintains a false sense that some land is more important than other land and is based on human wants and desires rather than an understanding and respect for the larger ecology of an area. Obviously, such a practice and perspective offers no recognition of ecosystem function or concern for species' survival. Yet, in order to preserve any land, strategically, groups must support such swaps.

Ultimately, whether on the property rights or environmentalist side of the debates around land and development, many of us do not recognize ourselves and our livelihoods with reference to the larger, less aesthetic, less "useful" world; and our social structures, like the legislative process, discourage us from viewing land in a way other than in terms of its use-value.

PUTTING A LAND ETHIC TO PRACTICE

If sprawl is a product of a rationalized, mechanical, individualistic, consumerist, and litigious orientation to land, then, to help guide us out of the sprawl dilemma, we may look toward communities that exhibit a land ethic and demonstrate meaning-based, fluid, and cooperative orientations to land. Various communities worldwide have deliberately and thoughtfully put a land ethic to practice. Furthermore, numerous communities have resisted the modern industrial drive to sever traditional symbolic connections to land and have maintained a land ethic even amidst rampant overdevelopment. Several examples of such communities in America discussed below help us to see the possibilities for creating such relationships with land. And in the words of journalist Dero A. Saunders, "If it exists, it's possible" (The Painter's Keys 2006).

Many towns and cities throughout America are in the process of building a larger sense of community and reconnecting to the land that sustains us. The use of local money, the local food movement, and local permaculture projects are just a few examples of collective community action designed to rebuild connections with the land and each other. Through the creation of their own local currency, currency intended for trade within small areas and not financially backed by the federal government, more than 2,500 towns nationally have created community-trading systems (Rayner 2006). Aside from supporting their town's economy, using local money connects residents with local food sources and makes them cognizant of the direct effects their lifestyles have upon the land. The local food movement encourages residents to purchase food produced within close range of their neighborhoods. This may come in the form of food co-ops where community members purchase food from local farms or community gardens in which families combine to cultivate a plot of land and share the produce. In this way, community members learn to rely once again on the land for their sustenance and become more conscious of how to live sustainably on that land. Permaculture, based on the principles of living holistically with the land, supports gardening designed to balance soils, plants, animals, and humans so that the land thrives and becomes, once again, self-sustainable.

Ecovillages—communities of people who strive to live socially, economically, and ecologically sustainable lives—are designed to prevent ecological disaster and counter sprawl, over-consumption, natural habitat destruction, and dependence on fossil fuels. Dozens of ecovillages now exist in rural and urban areas throughout the United States. They typically maintain populations of between 50 and 150 individuals and are designed to work in harmony with the surrounding bioregion, while accounting for water availability, the ability to grow food, and accessibility. To provide for most of the community needs, ecovillages usually depend on renewable energy, local purchasing, local food, and a consensus decision-making process. They maintain a focus on biological and cultural diversity and often practice permaculture, autonomous building methods (building off the "grid"), cluster development, and co-housing (individual dwellings with common facilities), or other forms of supportive community building.

East Lake Commons, an ecovillage in Atlanta, Georgia, has successfully used cluster development to preserve half of its eighteen-acre land base. Land that would have been developed into individual lots has been preserved as common open spaces. Five acres of organic gardens produce vegetables, flowers, herbs, and fruits for market. As with many ecovillages, courses are offered to the public on such topics as organic gardening, composting, rebuilding soils, and land planning in an ecovillage.

Ecovillages rely on sustainable building practices to develop their village structures. The SONG Neighborhood (Second Neighborhood Group) within the Ecovillage at Ithaca consists of fifteen duplexes, built on 3.5 acres. Eighteen acres are preserved as open space. Sustainable building practices include passive solar design, photovoltaics, solar hot water, high-efficiency condensing gas boilers, Eco-Block foundations, highly insulated panels and roofs, straw bale insulation, rainwater collection, composting toilets, drain heat recovery, and salvaged materials.

The Los Angeles Ecovillage, an example of an urban ecovillage, is located on just two city blocks. The ecovillage is integrated into an already existing neighborhood, and of the five hundred residents living on the two blocks, seventy-five participate in ecovillage activities and thirty-five have intentionally moved to the village. Half of the ecovillage members no longer drive cars and the community aims to serve as an example of how urban sustainability can operate within a sprawling metropolis. Community potluck dinners and workshops on permaculture and approaches to sustainable urban living are a few of the public services offered.

Many traditional communities have also resisted the pressures of the growth society. The Salt River Pimas have a land ethic built into their culture. Although many of their traditions have been obliterated (largely through forced assimilation and sustained economic pressures), a widespread effort to preserve a land ethic through memory and tradition acts as a counterforce to the dominant growth model. Preserving land on which future generations may live holds great meaning and importance to Pima families. Providing land for future generations has shaped the way the Pimas traditionally structure their rancherias, spread far enough away from each other to sustain growing families. The land, as home, guards, cares for, and protects the Pimas. "You know land is forever. You use it. You take care of it just like you would an animal—your horses, your wagon team," says Pam. She explains that when suppertime arrives, your horse is even hungrier than you are. You need to feed the horse before you feed yourself. It is the same with the land. "Take care of the land. We do not sell it somewhere down the road. You can't go and live out there. You got no roots out there. The land will always be there—you can always feel you have a home. Maybe it's not a fancy home, but at least you'll have a roof over your head."

Henry, a Native man who has worked in the Salt River Community, explains that no matter what laws are passed or if they are moved off this land, or even if Phoenix grows over their land, to the Pima this land will always be sacred. Even today, their love of the land extends beyond the artificial borders placed around them. They sing to the land and remember landmarks through song. Their entire way of life stems from the land.

A Pima legend holds that the roadrunner's "strong legs helped to 'fold up the earth' (make good time)" (Shaw 1968:95). Carrie, a young Pima college student, recalls this legend as she wonders how the freeway "folds up the earth" so that we may make good time. She, like many others, draws on her culture's legends and traditions to look critically at land development in her community.

In my conversations with elders, I learned that many maintain traditional connections with the land through growing their own vegetables and beans and cooking traditional foods. They also tell stories to their children and grandchildren about land and life on the reservation long ago. Young people tell me that they actively work to revive traditional rites, encouraging elders to teach them songs, prayers, and ceremonies.

While direct collective action with associated legal challenges characterizes many communities' approaches toward resisting suburban sprawl, the Pimas evoke powerful memories and traditions as forms of collective resistance. Memory does not serve as nostalgia, where one relives the past as if the past exists in a vacuum with no connection to the present or future. For Salt River residents, memory has a much more compelling effect. Memory brings past images and traditions to bear upon the present and shapes visions of the future.

Anthropologist David Scott (1999) identified tradition and memory as places of contention and challenge. Indigenous groups are in particularly unique positions to draw upon memory and tradition as challenges to systems of power that promote urbanization because, in many cases, they have lived and continue to live on the same land for many generations. In contrast, residents in most American communities tend to move and do not form such generational ties to the land.[4] Family land inheritances and maintenance of tradition are rare in American life.

The case of the Hopi Tribe is an example of a community that thinks outside of American political and economic structures and pursues economic development while preserving their love of land and the Hopi culture. The Hopi villages, located on top of three mesas in the semiarid desert of northern Arizona and surrounded by the Navajo Reservation, are the oldest continuously occupied settlements in the United States. The Hopis have maintained their ancient religious practices, clan family structures, language, medical knowledge, traditional foods, agricultural techniques, and fine arts, and they have never signed a treaty of any kind with the United States government. Maintaining tribal sovereignty and independence from American culture is deemed essential for maintaining the Hopi way of life. Several of the villages do not even recognize the Hopi tribal government, feeling that it acts as a puppet for the larger American government. These villages maintain their traditional governing system, led by the village chiefs, the Kikmongwis. Their traditionalism separates them from the larger dominant society.

Four of the twelve Hopi villages prohibit electrical power lines, enforcing the feeling that electricity from generating plants damages the environment and may threaten tribal sovereignty. Leaders from these villages are concerned that the Hopi people will get hooked on an American materialist way of thinking and lose sight of their role as stewards of the land and of life. As one Hopi elder, Thomas Banyacya (1976), explains, "Traditional Hopi follow the spiritual path that was given to us by Massau'u the Great Spirit. We made a sacred covenant to follow his life plan, . . . taking care of this land and life. Our goals are not to gain political control or monetary wealth, but to pray and to promote the welfare of all living beings and to preserve the world in a natural way." The Hopis believe that a fragile harmony holds human beings, the earth, and nature together. Banyacya further explains,

Through Hopi prophecy and spiritual beliefs the Hopi know that greed, pollution and lack of understanding of nature are about to destroy Mother Earth. The Hopi and all Native Brothers have continually struggled in their existence to maintain harmony with the earth and with the universe. To the Hopi, land is sacred; and if the land is abused, the sacredness of Hopi life will disappear and all other life as well. Land is the foundation of Hopi and all life.

Village leaders feel that the energy from power lines could interfere with ceremonial areas and also interfere with the laws of nature. The Hopi Foundation explains that "the force field of electricity emanating from the power lines is considered to be disruptive to the atmosphere, ambiance, and balance of the plaza ceremonial areas, at the same time blocking the aesthetics of the sky and the panoramic vistas of the mesas" (Hopi Information Network 1999).

Photovoltaics (technology that, when exposed to light, produces voltage) have connected reverence for the sun and Earth with modern industrial needs. Through photovoltaic solar panels, sunlight is captured on the roofs of homes to provide electricity. There are no power lines and no outside utility companies involved. The Native Sun Hopi Solar Electric Enterprise, a nonprofit company developed and run by Hopis, provides solar power to families at a reasonable cost. Hopis and Navajos can apply for low-interest loans to purchase and install photovoltaic systems on their homes. Since nearly fifty percent of Hopi and Navajo homes do not have electricity, and often rely on kerosene and propane lamps to provide light, photovoltaics provides an environmentally sound alternative. The use of photovoltaics eliminates the need for outside utilities, is more reliable than utility lines that get knocked down by snow and winds, and encourages locally run enterprises.

The Hopi use of photovoltaics illustrates an economically viable, environmentally healthy alternative while preserving and meeting the cultural needs of the community. Furthermore, the Hopis serve as an example of how a committed community may be self-reliant and thrive outside of environmentally destructive dominant cultural and structural arrangements.

Alternative perceptions and approaches to land—like using local money, purchasing local food, developing permaculture

Cave Creek.

projects—and examples of communities that embrace a land ethic—like ecovillages and the Pima and the Hopi—suggest that land preservation is not simply about imposing laws but comes through deep and enduring connections with the land. Leopold wrote, "Obligations have no meaning without conscience, and the problem we face is the extension of the social conscience from people to land" (1949:246). Responsibility entails a commitment to choosing to walk along a particular path despite one's desires, enticements, and fears. Responsibility is not based on one group's demands over another group and their values turned into law. Responsibility is the recognition of something greater than the self. It may entail love and care for your own land and recognition that private lands are also part of a larger ecosystem that transcends private borders, and that in certain cases groups instead of individuals might better serve that land.

A land ethic sets the stage for preservation of land not because we need such things as the watershed of forests to serve our irrigation needs (Hayes 1959), not even because we need to preserve something wild so that our children will know more than the concrete jungles that engulf many of their lives. Development of a land ethic is not really about *us* at all, though it is not devoid of our needs either. A land ethic is essential because without it we cannot truly understand why the knowledge that three new malls go up every hour and 228 acres of land get developed every hour *hurts*. Development of a land ethic is necessary because it makes paving over more land intolerable, and without it all kinds of excuses are made for sprawl.

Conclusion

Driving north, past the Salt River Community, past Cave Creek and Spur Cross Ranch, I arrive at my destination. Although we have taken a few detours through suburban sprawl with its tamed lawns, artificial washes, toxins, and miles of asphalt, there are places left—places that defy our attempts to dominate and control. We have yet to figure out a way to make it economically feasible to bring our urban infrastructures to all parts of the desert. I wander through groves of mesquite and cottonwoods growing in thickets along dry washes. Towering sycamore trees extend into the big sky. I listen to their crinkling leaves as a slight breeze brushes through them and I choose one to sit beneath. Wildflower shoots encircle me. One with vibrant green leaves captures my attention and I take in its color for what seems like the first time.

I linger beneath these generous arms, feeling the sycamore as my protector, at least for a short while. The old tree offers its shade unconditionally; the colors of the desert floor intensify as the sun ducks behind a cloud; bird chatter comes in fits and bursts; and I sit in awe, beholding the mystery that unfolds before me and knowing that somehow I too unfold and participate in this eternal moment.

Had I walked ten miles west, I would have come across a fleet of tractors that scrape these lands "clean" to make room for a new subdivision. And when I witness this, I feel great pain. The earth bleeds and I too feel uprooted, displaced.

Nature holds great lessons for us all, and when we destroy these lands, we lose great teachers. As I sit beneath the sycamore

with its craggy branches, some bare and scorched by wind and age, I envision the deformed fingers of an old lady and I understand the beauty that resides in the aged. The old tree stands magnificent in its imperfection. Our elderly appear decrepit to us because we have lost our ability to *see*. The heat of the desert sun burns cottonwood leaves that form the cushion upon which I sit. A red-tailed hawk circles above me while two jets mark their linear paths across the deep blue Arizona sky.

Blading the land for profit has widespread and unforeseen consequences. We need wild places. Wild places stir our souls, helping us to see and guiding us without judgment to wild places within ourselves. I know of no one who has received this kind of wisdom from a sprawling master-planned community.

I look across miles of desert, pulsating with life and beauty, and think to myself: "These lands don't need to be paved over." I hear the opposite message from nearly all with whom I have spoken over the past ten years. They tell me that sprawl is inevitable. Even the most avid environmentalist says that his job is merely to stop the D-9 bulldozers for one more day. The

Replanting saguaros.

powerful forces of land development, he concludes, will eventually conquer these lands.

My entire being resists what everyone else calls "reality." I am called an "idealist." But whatever the label, I see the land as it is now and right now there are sparrows singing songs, and great rocky banks, and a roadrunner that continues to evade my sight as it disappears into scraggly brush and prickly cactus. I see a dozen shades of yellow, one of which I have seen only here in the scorched grasses of the Sonoran Desert.

What becomes of these lands is our collective choice. We need not choose a destructive path and resign ourselves to believing that this is the only path. There is no doubt that the dominant power structures, as they currently exist, support continued sprawl. Yet by playing the power game, largely through lawsuits and land purchases, we reinforce the dominant power structure that says in order to preserve, we need to play by the rules—which by their very nature support the growth society.

There is no one correct answer, no one approach to curbing sprawl. Some must continue to directly challenge the forces of

Spur Cross Ranch, undeveloped.

authority and influence in our society and use all of the tools of this society to do so. Yet whether challenging sprawl through no-growth boundaries, regional planning, land trusts, or cluster development, we must also address why we sprawl in the first place.

Collectively, we must examine the recesses of our own consciousness, our myths, and our social constructions while imagining and experimenting with new ways of living. In the process of this personal and collective exploration, a deep collective reflection, *we will change*, and our patterns of living will change.

From my own personal reflections, I have decided to learn the art and science of permaculture, and together with my daughter, create a garden based on the principles of living holistically with the land. *This is social change.* Social change occurs in our own backyards and in enlarging our sense of our own backyards. Social change occurs as we collectively seek alternative models and alternative stories for living.

We have examined several key cultural forces of suburban sprawl, all of which assume that nature is essentially separate from ourselves. If we comprehend and embrace the reality that all is in flux, ever changing, richly dynamic, and interconnected, we will seek new ways of living—ways that respect the land and ourselves as ever-evolving, inherently mysterious creations. Through limiting nature to something that requires our control, we have created a built environment that reflects this view of reality. Sprawl is the by-product of a belief system that views the land, community, and ourselves as inherently disconnected and in need of acute management.

An ant tumbles over tiny rocks, zigzagging its way through grass and seed and dust. A bumblebee casing lies midway through the process of decomposition, soon to become part of the soil. Its relative circles my head and then buzzes high above the trees. A crow squawks and glides across the sky. I rub my hands to create a little warmth as the sun begins to set and the desert quickly releases its heat. Cactus wrens flutter overhead, busily chattering about something that seems deeply important to them, though I shall never understand what that is. The mystery remains and I merely bear witness.

Appendix

Research Overview

My research focused on cultural perceptions of land and urbanization in Cave Creek, Arizona, and the Salt River Pima–Maricopa Indian Community. Research methods were designed to uncover community members' perceptions and responses to environmental change as well as the underlying cultural dynamics that influence these perceptions.

To understand environmental perceptions, I conducted interviews with twenty-seven individuals in each community (fifty-four interviews total). Interviews with community leaders also provided insight into the structural dynamics of the communities. An additional ten interviews were conducted with planners and developers in the Phoenix metropolitan area. I used a stratified sample based on age, gender, socioeconomic class, and degree of involvement in local government. Most interviews were obtained through recommendations from participants regarding other individuals who could offer a perspective on land and development different from their own. I asked participants open-ended questions regarding their thoughts on the desert and housing development.

Eugene Halton (1992) has called for putting the "cult" back into our concepts of "culture." He defined culture as the "living impulse to meaning" and criticized the abstract use of the term "culture." Through his notion of "bodied sign practices," Halton proposed a more expressive and connected exploration of how signs convey real meaning in real people's lives. I sought to apply Halton's notion by grounding culture in its particulars and understanding how meaning is constructed through human activity. I did this primarily through approaching interviews as discussions. These were not one-way question/answer sessions, but rather conversations where participants interacted with me, asked me questions, and engaged in both formal and informal conversation. The conversational nature of the interviews broke down barriers and helped me delve beyond information and into the feelings behind individual's ideas. By keeping Halton's "living impulse to meaning" in mind, I tried to remain sensitive to the way ideas operated in people's daily lives and the meaning they attached to their ideas.

To further understand cultural influences and gain insight into broader community and power dynamics, including the influence of economic forces and social and political institutions, I observed each community for three months (for a total of six months of observation) and continued periodic observations from 1996 through 2004.

The physical location of a researcher in a community affects community dynamics. The very presence of a researcher has an effect on how community members behave. I sought to remain as unobtrusive as possible when conducting observations. Although I had no conversations with community members regarding how they perceived me, I suspect that Cave Creek residents thought that I was a local tourist. Sam Minkler photographed each community while I conducted interviews. We dressed informally and I waited until afterward to take notes so it would not be obvious that I was conducting research. My presence within the Salt River Community was more noticeable. As that community does not attract tourists, we did not blend in with any group. Additionally, the local paper ran an announcement informing community members of my study. Many residents knew of my research and welcomed the opportunity to talk about land and development.

Skepticism about social research is understandably pervasive in Native communities. Residents often feel used by academia for little reward. Native Americans have historically been objectified and treated as anomalies whose rites and practices are observed as strange, mystical, or extraordinary. In essence, Native communities have been treated as the "other" by the academic community; they have been viewed as objects to be studied and so have been dehumanized. Given this history, it is important that social researchers obtain consent from tribes before conducting any such research. I therefore presented a research proposal to the Salt River tribal council and attended a tribal council meeting to address any questions or concerns they might have; the council then offered their consent for me to conduct this study. The Community manager wrote a letter of introduction on tribal stationary that I showed to each potential participant.

Although I am not Native American, I believe that Sam, as a Navajo, helped me gain further access to members of the Salt River Community. While Sam is clearly not Pima, community members joked around with me, called me their "in-law," and seemed intrigued by my own interest in Native land issues. Furthermore, I was in my second trimester of pregnancy when I interviewed Salt River residents. I believe that being a young pregnant woman may have broken certain barriers—especially with other women. Female participants often asked me questions about my pregnancy or related stories of their own experiences with pregnancy before the interview. This helped to create an atmosphere where participants seemed relaxed and spoke easily and frankly with me.

My analysis of newspaper articles from three papers (January 1996 to December 1998) focused on environment and development issues. I analyzed 458 articles from the *Arizona Republic*, the primary daily newspaper for the state of Arizona; 250 articles from the *Sonoran News*, one of two popular weekly papers in Cave Creek; and 46 articles from *Au-Authm Action News*, the main monthly paper for the Salt River Pima–Maricopa Indian Community. I analyzed an additional 25 editorials from the *Arizona Republic* from 2002 to 2003.

Analysis of interviews, observations, and newspapers took a grounded theory approach that allows theoretical connections to emerge and reduces the possibilities for placing preconceptions on the analysis. I used a qualitative research computer program to aid in the coding of all data. After each interview I took analytic memos, highlighting key themes expressed by the interviewee. Next, I transcribed the interview and coded it for key themes. As new codes arose, I returned to previously coded interviews to see how those ideas did or did not get reflected. In this way I achieved distance from the material, then returned to it in order to ground ideas in concrete spoken words. After a comprehensive process of coding, recoding, and revisiting all interviews, after coding all articles, and after analyzing six months of observations, I arrived at five cultural forces that drive sprawl. These cultural forces are limited to the case studies, but an extensive literature review suggests that they also apply to the broader dominant culture. I have thus used the case studies as illustrative of certain cultural dynamics that appear more broadly in American society.

Aside from coding and identifying themes, I also took a deconstructionist approach to analyzing interviews and news articles. To Jacques Derrida (1974), words always carry "traces" of other words in texts and can thus be "deconstructed" to unravel their truth claims. What we write or say as "fact" must be seen within the socio-economic-political-cultural context in which it was written or said. In addition, words often reveal "double meanings" and hidden ones. This study deconstructs truth claims made by the many individuals and groups that compose the sprawl debate within the two communities and throughout the Phoenix metropolitan area. Through looking at the language of responsible development, for example, I have attempted to reveal its double meaning—how it is used to both resist and sustain sprawl.

NOTES

INTRODUCTION

1. Riparian areas define the edge between land and water. They filter pollutants, prevent erosion, and provide food and shelter to a large variety of animals.

2. Debate ensues regarding the nature of the "Sunbelt." The term was originally coined in 1969 by Kevin Phillips to refer to South and southwestern states that emerged after World War II as a new conservative constituency.

3. In the 2000 national elections, there were 209 ballot referendums around the country to support land conservation, largely through citizens taxing themselves. Eighty-three percent of those referendums were supported by a majority of votes. More than a million Americans currently contribute to conservation efforts on a local level (Forbes 2001:35).

4. "Ecological integrity" is "the ability of an ecosystem to function healthily and continue to provide natural goods and services and maintain biodiversity" (American Museum of Natural History).

5. In Arizona there are fifty-nine federally listed endangered species. These include seventeen plants, eighteen fish, eleven birds, nine mammals, two reptiles, a frog, and a snail. Some endangered species in Arizona symbolizing the Southwest include the Mexican gray wolf, jaguar, ocelot, Sonoran pronghorn antelope, Mexican spotted owl, Mt. Graham red squirrel, Colorado squawfish, ferruginous pygmy owl, Southwest willow flycatcher, and Huachuca water umbel (American Lung Association et al. 2000).

6. For an overview of structural causes of suburban sprawl, see Bullard et al. 2000; Duany et al. 2000; Partners for Livable Communities 2000; Razen 1998; Weatherby and Witt 1994.

7. R. G. Collingwood (1945/1960) held that, without understanding the whole history of Western thought, one cannot grasp the term "nature." Nature has been defined as anything material, as "boundless," as "kosmos," as something internal that makes its possessor behave in a certain way, as geometric form, and so on. Aristotle defined nature as origin, the seed from which all things grow, primitive matter, essence of form, process, growth, change and movement, something that changes in a particular way until it reaches its goal. The dualist tradition, epitomized by Descartes and including Spinoza, Newton, Leibniz, and Locke, viewed nature as everything except the mind. The idealist or mentalist tradition believed that nature as a whole is the work of the mind. Others such as Whitehead held that nature was not merely an organism but a process.

CHAPTER 1: THE RATIONAL SOCIETY

1. Most literature written on the Hoo-hoogam spell it "Hohokam," but I use the Pima spelling, "Hoo-hoogam."

2. This population figure may have been low due to inconsistent tallying (Ezell 1983).

3. Salt River Community enterprises include Salt River Gaming Enterprises, Talking Stick Golf Course, Salt River Commercial Landfill Enterprises, Salt River Sand and Rock Company, Cypress Golf Course, Red Mountain Trap and Skeet, Saddleback Communications Company, and Salt River DEVCO Asset Management.

4. Throughout this book I refer to the unfortunate artificial categories of Western and indigenous societies. These categories are somewhat problematic in that they overlook the fact that no society lives isolated from all other societies. In addition, indigenous cultures do not exist in areas separate from Western cultures. Thus, to talk about the West as if indigenous groups are not part of this geographic area is a misnomer. Nonetheless, certain cultural experiences are shared by people of European and American descent (the West), and by indigenous cultures that descend from populations present before modern borders were defined and that maintain their traditional socio-political-economic ways of life.

5. Nicolaus Copernicus (1473–1543) directly observed this sensory deception when he discerned that the Earth moves around the sun, despite our experience of the sun and stars moving while the earth remains still. In 1571, Johannes Kepler used mathematics as the basis for directly measuring observations, offering the tools for scientific empirical analysis.

6. Newton's laws of motion hold that (1) all objects move with constant velocity unless an outside force acts on them, (2) force equals mass times acceleration (this tells us how much effect an outside force has on an object), and (3) for every action there is an equal and opposite reaction.

7. Newton has been used as a symbol of the overrationalized society and the inhumane outcomes that have resulted. However, in *Issac Newton*, James Gleik (2003) writes that Newton the man was far more complex and never felt he had a complete system of the world. Gleik holds that while today we deem Newton the father of modern science, Newton himself was both a scientist and a mystic. Charles Murray (2003) held that a latent consequence of Newton's science of motion has been the application of this to human societies. "Man could remake the world from scratch by designing new human institutions through the application of scientific reason." This trust in reason led to such toxic undertakings as the Jacobin Republic, Leninism, and Stalinism, and I would add the Nazi program to exterminate all Jews. Drawing on these thoughts, I do not analyze Newton the scientist here, but the principles of rationality and predictability that have influenced our built environment, often in detrimental ways.

8. Jefferson designed American townships to be one hundred square miles each. Thirty-six square-mile townships were adopted in 1785. "The difference between the two [township designs] fades into insignificance compared with the shared ideal of rationality, proportion, and orderly process. Social harmony itself

was and is believed to be the fruit of rationality—of 'order of the land' " (Tuan 1993:148).

9. The relationship between compromised ecology and increased disease and social problems is explored in Awiakta 1993, Ehrenfeld 2002, Kohm 1991, Hoff and McNutt 1994, Shiva 1994, Suzuki and McConnell 1999, Swan and Swan 2000, Hertsgaard 1998.

10. The environmental justice movement attempts to address these injustices. See Weaver 1997; Camacho 1998; Adamson, Evans and Stein 2002.

CHAPTER 2: CULTURAL PRODUCTIONS OF TIME AND SPACE

1. See Certeau et al. 1998; Doxtater 2005; Hall 1966; Harvey 1989; Lefebvre 1991; Low and Lawrence-Zúñiga 1900, 2003; Warner and Molotch 2001; Zerubavel 1991, 1997.

2. See Harvey 1989; Hochschild 1997; Lefebvre 2004; Nippert-Eng 1996; Zerubavel 1981, 1985, 2003.

3. Traditional societies do not merely organize space and time cyclically. Some Native American landscapes, for example, are arranged georitually (Doxtater 2005) and symbolic and religious landmarks act as central organizing points.

4. As Vine Deloria, Jr., wrote, "Luther Standing Bear once remarked that people had to be born, reborn, and reborn again on a piece of land before beginning to come to grips with its rhythms" (1991:32).

5. The "Ecological Footprint" calculates how much land and water an individual uses, based on location globally and lifestyle. Take the "Earthday Footprint Quiz" to calculate your ecological footprint: http://www.earthday.net/footprint/info.asp.

CHAPTER 3: SELLING "THE AMERICAN DREAM"

1. *Boston*: "In 1773, the only visitors arriving to Boston's shores were the English Redcoats. Today, Bostonians welcome more than 10 million visitors each year from all over the world as they arrive in Boston to enjoy this exciting and interesting city" (City of Boston visitor's page; http://www.ci.boston.ma.us/vistors/default.asp; retrieved February 3, 2002).

Buffalo: "The City of Good Neighbors." "the city that's easy to love." Another promo reads: "Buffalo is a city with a rich history and a promising future. We have weathered the economic turbulence caused by the demise of our heavy manufacturing industries that employed the bulk of out [*sic*] workers and are now poised to market the same strategic geography that led to Buffalo's boom period as the catalyst to a new era of growth and prosperity" (City of Buffalo homepage; http://www.ci.buffalo.ny.us/document_3.html; retrieved February 2, 2002).

Hartford, Conn.: "During the American colonial era, James II, king of England, repealed the charter of the colony of Connecticut. When Sir Edmund Andros was dispatched in 1687 to Hartford, Connecticut, to retrieve the document, he found it to have been hidden by Captain John Wadsworth, who had sequestered it in an oak tree" (City of Hartford homepage; http://www.ci.hartfor.ct.us; retrieved February 3, 2002).

2. *Atlanta*: "Welcome to Possibility City—Anything is Possible" (City of Atlanta homepage; http://www.ci.atlanta.ga.us; retrieved February 2, 2002).

Jacksonville, Fla.: "If you take a look around Jacksonville, you'll see why journalists are raving. Our city is 840 square miles of pure pleasure" (City of Jacksonville homepage; http://www.coj.net/pub/citygov/mayor.html; retrieved February 3, 2002).

Miami: "Exciting-Electrifying-Enchanting-Exhilarating" (City of Miami visitor's page; http://www.ci.miami.fl.us/visitor.htm; retrieved February 2, 2002).

Norfolk: "Life. Celebrate Daily" (City of Norfolk homepage). You've come for a fun-filled time, so make sure you visit Norfolk's attractions and restaurants during your stay, and plan to attend our special celebrations throughout the city" (City of Norfolk welcome page; http://www.Norfolk.va.us; retrieved February 3, 2002).

3. *Cincinnati*: "Greater Cincinnati is home to almost 2 million people. It features all the amenities of a large, bustling metropolis while maintaining a friendly, small town atmosphere" (Greater Cincinnati Chamber of Commerce, "About Us"; http://www.gccc.com/about_Cincinnati; retrieved February 3, 2002).

Columbus, Ohio: "This area is as exciting and vibrant as any in America, yet it retains the values and characteristics that we hold dear in Columbus—A city where people care about each other . . . where we enjoy a high quality of life and celebrate city to the next level." State of the City address, February 22, 2001, by Mayor Michael B. Coleman (http://mayor.ci.Columbus.oh.us/state_of_the_city_2001.htm; retrieved February 2, 2002).

Kansas City, Mo.: "Welcome to Kansas City, City of Fountains, city of *fun* . . . whether doing business, raising a family, cheering the home-town team or looking for a night on the town, Greater Kansas City stacks up . . . Discover why we in Kansas City really are *living the good life*" (Kansas City Chamber of Commerce; http://www.kcchamber.com/coming2kc/coming2kc.htm; retrieved February 2, 2002).

4. *Portland, Ore.*: Its byline is the "city that works" (City of Portland homepage, my emphasis; http://www.ci.portland.or.us; retrieved February 2, 2002).

5. Robert Putnam (2000) finds that social and political engagement in America has declined within the last third of the twentieth century.

CHAPTER 4: CONSUMING THE DREAM

1. The U.S. Census Bureau News (2005) reports that "during the past decade, the fastest-growing region was the West at 19.7 percent, which added 10.4 million people in the 1990s for a total of 63.2 million. The fastest-growing states in the nation were all located in the West: Nevada (66.3 percent), Arizona (40.0 percent), Colorado (30.6 percent), Utah (29.6 percent) and Idaho (28.5 percent). California recorded the largest numeric increase of any state, 4.1 million people."

2. All quotes are from http://www.immigrationresource.org/about_need.html: "The influx of newcomers has brought indirect urban renewal, reversing the blight that threatened New York in the 1970s and helping to avoid serious inner-city population loss that has plagued such cities as Philadelphia and Detroit."

"Immigrants have been crucial to maintaining not only the city's population, but also its housing stock" (*The Newest New Yorkers 1995–1996*, New York City Department of City Planning).

"Many [immigrants] are opening businesses not traditionally associated with immigrants and helping to reshape industries and revitalize neighborhoods. The result has been a flowering of small businesses in areas traditionally favored by immigrants as well as in new niches such as construction, travel and franchising" (Ernst & Young's Kenneth Leventhal Real Estate Group, May 1998).

"This continuing strong influx of human capital into New York City is a key ingredient of our economic strength and of the revitalization of many neighborhoods. . . . New York City's continued welcome to immigrants has allowed it to thrive while many other older cities have not" (Joseph B. Rose, chairman of the New York City Planning Commission).

CHAPTER 5: RIGHTS WARS AND DEVELOPING A LAND ETHIC

1. The Fourteenth Amendment, Section 1, states: "nor shall any state deprive any person of life, liberty, or property, without due process of law; nor deny to any person within its jurisdiction the equal protection of the laws."

2. Ray Anderson, CEO of the global commercial interior company Interface, has committed his company to achieve 100 percent sustainability by 2020. He has laid out a path to achieve this and Interface is showing the world how, with a committed vision, a petroleum-dependent industry can transform itself. Anderson believes that sustainable industry is possible and is the key to staving off global ecological disaster. See Interface Sustainability at http://www.interfacesustainability.com.

3. The term "environmental triage" borrows from the French term "triage"— a picking out, sorting, from the Old French *trier*: to pick. In World War I, nurses "triaged" injured soldiers into three groups, according to the severity of their wounds. First treated were soldiers who were not expected to die, with or without aid (Barnahart 1995:831).

4. As Paula Gunn Allen has explained, "The Native American sense of the importance of continuity with one's cultural origins runs counter to contemporary American ideas: in many instances, the immigrants to America have been eager to cast off cultural ties, often seeing their antecedents as backward, restrictive, even shameful" (1986:649).

References

This list includes both references cited in the book and additional sources consulted.

Abbey, Edward. 1988. *Desert Solitaire*. Tucson: University of Arizona Press.

Acuff, Guy. 1980. *A Kimult Aw A Tham: The River People; A Short History of the Pima Indians*. Casa Grande, Ariz.: Casa Grande Printing.

Adamson, Joni, Mei Mei Evans, and Rachel Stein, eds. 2002. *The Environmental Justice Reader: Politics, Poetics, and Pedagogy*. Tucson: University of Arizona Press.

Allen, Paula Gunn. 1986. "Who Is Your Mother? Red Roots of White Feminism." In *Social Theory: The Multicultural and Classical Readings*, edited by Charles Lemert. 1993, 648–53. San Francisco: Westview Press.

American Lung Association of Arizona, Arizona Audubon Council, Arizona Heritage Alliance, Arizona Public Health Association, Center for Biological Diversity, Citizens for Growth Management, and Grand Canyon Trust, Sierra Club–Grand Canyon Chapter. January 12, 2000. *State of the Environment Arizona*.

American Museum of Natural History. Center for Biodiversity and Conservation. Glossary. http://research.amnh.org/biodiversity/symposia/archives/seascapes/glossary.html (retrieved May 16, 2005).

Archer, John. 1988. "Ideology and Aspiration: Individualism, the Middle Class and the Genesis of the Anglo-American Suburb." *Journal of Urban History* 14 (2): 214–53.

Arendt, Randall. 1994. *Rural by Design: Maintaining Small Town Character*. Chicago, Ill.: Planners' Press: American Planning Association.

Arigoni, Danielle. 2001. *Affordable Housing and Smart Growth: Making the Connection*. Washington, D.C.: National Neighborhood Coalition.

Arizona Department of Environmental Quality. January 11, 2001. "Arizona Governor's Brown Cloud Summit Final Report." http://ww.adeq.state.az.us/environ/air/browncloud/index.html (retrieved January 29, 2001).

Arizona Republic. 2001. Section E. March 17.

Arizona Republic. May 11, 2003. "Residential Growth Pushes Edge of Phoenix to New Frontiers." Smart Growth News section.

Arizona Secretary of State. September 2000. "2000 Ballot Propositions: Proposition 100." http://www.sosaz.com/election/2000/info/pubpamphlet/english/prop100.htm (retrieved September 17, 2004).

REFERENCES

Arizona State Land Department. "Annual Report 1999–2000."
Au-Authm Action News. January 1996–December 1998. Salt River Pima–Maricopa Indian Community.
Awiakta, Marilou. 1993. *Selu: Seeking the Corn-Mother's Wisdom*. Mary Adair. Golden, Colo.: Fulcrum.
Bahr, Donald, J. Smith, W. S. Allison, and J. Hayden. 1994. *The Short Swift Time of Gods on Earth: The Hohokam Chronicles*. Los Angeles: University of California Press.
Bahr, Donald, Lloyd Paul, and Vincent Joseph. 1997. *Ant and Orioles: Showing the Art of Pima Poetry*. Salt Lake City: University of Utah Press.
Banyacya, Thomas. 1976. "Jo-Vow-Ma-Techgua Ikachi (Gathering) (Land) (My Life)." Presented to Chairman and members of the United Nations assembled in Vancouver, B.C., Canada. June 11.
Barnahart, Robert K., ed. 1995. *The Barnhart Concise Dictionary of Etymology*. New York: HarperCollins.
Baudrillard, Jean. 1970/1998. *The Consumer Society: Myths and Structures*. London: Sage Publications.
————. 1988/1989. *America*. New York: Verso.
Bellah, Robert N., Richard Madsen, William M. Sullivan, Ann Swidler, and Steven M. Tipton. 1985/1996. *Habits of the Heart: Individualism and Commitment in American Life*. Berkeley: University of California Press.
Benedict, Ruth. 1927/2001. *O'Odham Creation and Related Events*. As told to Ruth Benedict in 1927. In *Prose, Oratory, and Song*, edited by Donald Bahr. Tucson: University of Arizona Press.
Blaine, Thomas W., and Peggy Shear. 2005. "Ohio State University Fact Sheet: Cluster Development." http://ohioline.osu.edu/cd-fact/1270.html (retrieved April 30, 2005).
Boyer, M. Christine. 1983. *Dreaming the Rational City: The Myth of American City Planning*. Cambridge, Mass.: MIT Press.
Brundtland Commission Report. 1987. *Our Common Future*. Report of the UN World Commission on Environment and Development. Oxford, U.K.: Oxford University Press.
Bullard, Robert D., Glenn S. Johnson, and Angel O. Torres. 2000. *Sprawl City: Race, Politics and Planning in Atlanta*. Washington, D.C.: Island Press.
Camacho, David, ed. 1998. *Environmental Injustices, Political Struggles: Race, Class, and the Environment*. Durham, N.C.: Duke University Press.
Carlisle, John. 1999. "The Campaign against Urban Sprawl: Declaring War on the American Dream." *National Policy Analysis*. A publication of the National Center for Public Policy Research, April. http://www.nationalcenter.org/NPA239 .html (retrieved August 29, 1999).
Carlson, Frances. 1988. *Cave Creek and Carefree, Ariz.: A History of the Desert Foothills*. Scottsdale, Ariz.: Enchanto Press.
Certeau, Michel de; Luce Giard, and Pierre Mayol. 1998. *The Practice of Everyday Life*. Vol. 2: *Living and Cooking*. Minneapolis: University of Minnesota Press.

REFERENCES

City of Phoenix General Plan. June 26, 2001.

City of Scottsdale General Plan, November, 2001.

Christie, Les. 2006. "Fastest Growing Cities." CNNMoney.com. http://Money.cnn
.com/2006/06/20/real_estate/fastest_growing_cities/index.htm (retrieved January 12, 2008).

Clifford, James. 1992. "Traveling Cultures." In *Cultural Studies,* edited by Lawrence Grossberg, Cary Nelson, Paula Treichler, 96–116. New York: Routledge.

Collingwood, R. G. 1945/1960. *The Idea of Nature.* New York: Oxford University Press.

Coyle, Dennis J. 1993. *Property Rights and the Constitution: Shaping Society through Land Use Regulation.* Albany: State University of New York Press.

Cronon, William. 1995. "Introduction: In Search of Nature." In *Uncommon Ground: Toward Reinventing Nature,* edited by William Cronon, 23–56. New York: W. W. Norton.

Davis, Mike. 1992. *City of Quartz: Excavating the Future in Los Angeles.* New York: Vintage Books.

DC Ranch. "DC Ranch Vibrant and Growing." http://www.dcranch.com/ (retrieved January 24, 2006).

Deloria, Jr., Vine. 1991. "Reflection and Revelation: Knowing Land, Places, and Ourselves." In *The Power of Place: Sacred Ground in Natural & Human Environments: An Anthology,* edited by James A. Swan, 28–40. Wheaton, Ill.: Quest Books.

Del Webb homepage. http://www.delwebb.com (retrieved September 2002).

Derber, Charles. 1996. *The Wilding of America.* New York: St. Martin's Press.

————. 2000. *The Pursuit of Attention : Power and Ego in Everyday Life.* Oxford University Press.

Derrida, Jacques. 1974. *Of Grammatology.* Baltimore: John Hopkins University Press.

Descartes, Rene. 1641/1980. *Discourse on Method and Meditations on First Philosophy.* 1st ed. Indianapolis, Ind.: Hackett.

Destination Cinema. "Making Magic." http://destinationcinema.com/dci_news/pr.asp?id=121 (retrieved September 12, 2004).

DMB Associates. "Silverleaf." http://www.dmbinc.com/communities/desert.php (retrieved January 24, 2006).

Doxtater, Dennis. 2005. "A Chacoan Georitual Visiter Center on I-40." Paper presented at Conference: *Seeing the Past: Building Knowledge of the Past and Present through Acts of Seeing.* February 4–6. Stanford University. http://www
.metamedia.stanford.edu:3455/SeeingThePast/338 (retrieved December 1, 2006).

Duany, Andres, Elizabeth Plater-Zyberk, and Jeff Speck. 2000. *Suburban Nation: The Rise of Sprawl and the Decline of the American Dream.* New York: North Point Press.

Ehrenfeld, David. 2002. *Swimming Lessons: Keeping Afloat in the Age of Technology.* New York: Oxford University Press.

REFERENCES

Ezell, Paul. 1983. "History of the Pima." In *Handbook of North American Indians*, Vol. 10, 149–60. Washington D.C.: Smithsonian Institution.

Fiske, John. 1992. "Cultural Studies and the Culture of Everyday Life." In *Cultural Studies*, edited by Lawrence Grossberg, Cary Nelson, Paula Treichler, 154–73. New York: Routledge.

Foothills Community Foundation. 1990. *Carefree and Cave Creek Foothills: Life in the Sonoran Sun.* Cave Creek, Ariz.: Foothills Community Foundation.

Forbes, Peter. 2001. *The Great Remembering: Further Thoughts on Land, Soul and Society.* San Francisco: The Trust for Public Land.

Gans, Herbert. 1967. *The Levittowners: Ways of Life and Politics in a New Suburban Community.* New York: Vintage Books.

Garreau, Joel. 1988. *Edge City: Life on the New Frontier.* New York: Doubleday.

Geertz, C. 1973. "Deep Play: Notes on the Balinese Cockfight." In C. Geertz, *The Interpretation of Cultures*, 412–53. New York: Basic Books.

General Plan for Phoenix. 2004. "Executive Summary." http://phoenix.gov/ PLANNING/gpexec.html (retrieved September 17, 2004).

Gersh, Jeff. 1996. "Subdivide and Conquer: Concrete, Condos, and the Second Conquest of the American West." *The Amicus Journal*, Fall, 18 (3): 14–20.

Gila Heritage Park. 1998. Brochure funded by Arizona Humanities Council. Phoenix.

Gleik, James. 2003. Interview on "The Diane Rehm Show," National Public Radio, June 12.

Golfable.com. Maricopa County Arizona Golf Courses. http://www.golfable.com/ golfcourses/county/Maricopa_County_AZ (retrieved June 13, 2005).

Golf Industry Association. July, 2003. "Issues Affecting the GIA." http:// www.azgia.com/issues.html (retrieved January 26, 2006).

Golley, Frank B., and Juan Bellot, eds. 1999. "Planning As a Way of Achieving Sustainable Development." In *Rural Planning from an Environmental Systems Perspective*, 3–17. New York: Springer-Verlag.

Gómez, Arthur R. 2000. "A Comparative Look at National Parks." *Land in the American West: Private Claims and the Common Good.* Seattle: University of Washington Press.

Goodall, D. W., and R. A. Perry, eds. 1979. *Arid-Land Ecosystems: Structure, Functioning and Management.* New York: Cambridge University Press.

Gordon, Phil. "State of Our City 2005." http://phoenix.gov/mayor/speeches/ 2005city.html (retrieved January 2, 2006).

The Governor's Brown Cloud Summit–Final Report. January 16, 2001. Jane Dee Hull, governor; Ed Phillips, chairman. Phoenix.

Grand Canyon IMAX Theater. "Grand Canyon IMAX Movie." http://www .grandcanyonimaxtheater.com/ (retrieved September 12, 2004).

Greater Phoenix Chamber of Commerce. http://www.phoenixchamber.com/ VisitorInformation/ (retrieved December 19, 2005).

REFERENCES

Greenway, Robert. 1995. "Healing by the Wilderness Experience." In *Wild Ideas*, edited by David Rothernberg, 182–93. Minneapolis: University of Minnesota Press.

Gulliford, Andrew. 2000. *Sacred Objects and Sacred Places: Preserving Tribal Traditions*. Boulder, Colo.: University Press of Colorado.

Hackenberg, Robert A. 1983. "Pima and Papago Ecological Adaptations." In *Handbook of North American Indians*, Vol. 10, 161–77. Washington D.C.: Smithsonian Institution.

Hall, Edward T. 1966/1990. *The Hidden Dimension*. New York: Anchor Books.

Halton, Eugene. 1992. "The Cultic Roots of Culture." In *Theory of Culture*, edited by R. Munch and N. Smelser, 29–63. Los Angeles: University of California Press.

Haraway, Donna. 1989. *Primate Visions: Gender, Race, and Nature in the World of Modern Science*. New York: Routledge.

———. 1991. *Simians, Cyborgs, and Women: The Reinvention of Nature*. New York: Routledge.

Harvey, David. 1989. *The Condition of Postmodernity*. Cambridge, Mass.: Basil Blackwell, Inc.

Hayden, Dolores. 2004. Interview on "The Diane Rehm Show," National Public Radio, August 4.

Hayes, Samuel P. 1959/1969. *Conservation and the Gospel of Efficiency: The Progressive Conservation Movement, 1890–1920*. New York: Atheneum.

Hertsgaard, Mark. 1998. *Earth Odyssey: Around the World in Search of Our Environmental Future*. New York: Broadway Books.

Hertz, Edwin, Terry Haywood, and Larry T. Reynolds. 1990. "The Sunbelt Syndrome: Radical Individualism at the End of the American Dream." *Humanity and Society*, 14 (3): 257–79.

Hochschild, Arlie R. 1997. *The Time Bind: When Work Becomes Home and Home Becomes Work*. New York: Henry Holt and Company.

Hoff, Marie D., and John G. McNutt, eds. 1994. *The Global Environmental Crisis: Implications for Social Welfare and Social Work*. Aldershot, Hampshire, UK: Ashgate Publishing.

Hommann, Mary. 1993. *City Planning in America: Between Promise and Despair*. Westport, Conn.: Praeger.

Hopi Information Network. 1999. "Debbie Tewa: Building a Future with Her Community." http://www.infomagic.net/~abyte/hopi/news/solar.htm (retrieved December 2, 1999).

Howe, Elizabeth. 1994. *Acting on Ethics in City Planning*. New Brunswick, N.J.: Rutgers University Press.

Huxley, Aldous. 1932/1965. *Brave New World*. New York: Harper & Row.

Ingold, Tim. 2000. *The Perception of the Environment: Essays on Livelihood, Dwelling and Skill*. New York: Routledge.

Interface Sustainability. 2006. http://www.interfacesustainability.com (retrieved October 12, 2006).

REFERENCES

Jackson, Kenneth J. 1985. *Crabgrass Frontier: The Suburbanization of the United States*. New York: Oxford University Press.

Jasper, James M. 2000. *Restless Nation: Starting Over in America*. Chicago: University of Chicago Press.

Kaplan, Rachel, and Stephen Kaplan. 1989. *The Experience of Nature: A Psychological Perspective*. New York: Cambridge University Press.

Kern, Stephen. 1983. *The Culture of Time and Space 1880–1918*. Cambridge, Mass.: Harvard University Press.

Knox, Paul L., ed. 1988. "The Design Professions and the Built Environment in a Postmodern Epoch." In *The Design Professions and the Built Environment*, 1–11. New York: Nichols.

Kohm, Kathryn A., ed. 1991. *Balancing on the Brink of Extinction: The Endangered Species Act and Lessons for the Future*. Washington, D.C.: Island Press.

Kohn, Margaret. 2003. *Radical Space: Building the House of the People*. Ithaca, N.Y.: Cornell University Press.

Kowalewski, David. 2000. *Deep Power: The Political Ecology of Wilderness and Civilization*. Huntington, N.Y.: Nova Science Publishers.

Krueckeberg, Donald A., ed. 1983. Introduction to Planning History in the United States. New Brunswick, N.J.: Center for Urban Policy Research.

Kruse, Kevin M., and Thomas J. Sugrue, eds. 2006. *The New Suburban History* Princeton, N.J.: Princeton University Press.

Land Trust Alliance. "National Land Trust Census." http://www.lta.org/aboutlt/census.shtml (retrieved January 7, 2006).

Lawrence, D., and S. Low. 1990. "The Built Environment and Spatial Form." *Annual Review of Anthropology*, 19: 453–505.

———. 2003. *The Anthropology of Space and Place: Locating Culture*. Malden, Mass.: Blackwell Publishing.

Lefebvre, Henri. 1991. *The Production of Space*. Malden, Mass.: Blackwell Publishing.

———. 2004. *Rhythmanalysis: Space, Time and Everyday Life*. New York: Continuum.

Leo, Christopher, Mary Ann Beavis, Andrew Carver, and Robyne Turner. 1998. "Is Urban Sprawl Back on the Political Agenda? Local Growth Control, Regional Growth Management, and Politics." *Urban Affairs Review* 34 (2): 179–211.

Leopold, Aldo. 1949/1970. *A Sand County Almanac*. New York: Ballantine Books.

Lincoln Institute. 2003. *Making Sense of Place–Phoenix: The Urban Desert*. Phoenix: A Northern Lights Production.

Little, David. 1986. "Natural Rights and Human Rights: The International Imperative." In *Natural Rights and Natural Law: The Legacy of George Mason*, edited by Robert P. Davidow, 67–122. Farifax, Va.: George Mason University Press.

Logan, Michael F. 1995. *Fighting Sprawl and City Hall*. Tucson: University of Arizona Press.

Luckingham, Bradford. 1989. *Phoenix: The History of a Southwestern Metropolis*. Tucson: University of Arizona Press.

REFERENCES

Marcuse, Herbert. 1964. *One-Dimensional Man: Studies in the Ideology of Advanced Industrial Society*. Boston: Beacon Press.

Marzulla, Nancie G. Spring. 1995. "The Magic of Property Rights." *National Wilderness Institute Resource*. http://www.nwi.org/ResourceArticles/ MagicProperty.html (retrieved March 16, 2006).

McPherson, C. B. 1962. *The Political Theory of Possessive Individualism: Hobbes to Locke*. Oxford: Clarendon Press.

Merchant, Carolyn. 1980/1990. *The Death of Nature: Women, Ecology, and the Scientific Revolution*. New York: HarperSanFrancisco.

Minkler [Schipper], Janine. 2000. *This I See and My Heart So Hurts: Cultural Perceptions of Nature and Responses to Environmental Change as Seen through the Urbanization of the Sonoran Desert*. Ann Arbor, Mich.: UMI Dissertation Services.

Mirage Homes. 2006. http://www.miragehomes.com/ (retrieved January 24, 2006).

Momaday, N. Scott. 2005. "New Perspectives on the West." PBS series. http:// www.pbs.org/weta/thewest/program/episodes/one/ (retrieved April 5, 2005).

Mumford, Lewis. 161. *The City in History: Its Origins, Its Transformations, and Its Prospects*. New York: Harcourt Brace & World.

Murray, Charles. 2003. "Well, It Seemed Like a Good Idea at the Time." *New York Times*, Week in Review, November 30, pp. 1 and 3.

Nash, Roderick. 1967/1982. *Wilderness and the American Mind*, 3rd ed. New Haven, Conn.: Yale University Press.

————. 1989. *The Rights of Nature: A History of Environmental Ethics*. Madison: University of Wisconsin Press.

National Resources Inventory. 2002. Annual NRI. U.S. Department of Agriculture. http://www.nrcs.usda.gov/technical/land/nri02/ (retrieved December 18, 2005).

Natural Resources Defense Council. 2005. "Cities and Green Living: Smart Growth/Sprawl." http://www.nrdc.org/cities/smartGrowth/nsolve.asp (retrieved April 4, 2005).

Nicolaides, Becky M. 2002. *My Blue Heaven: Life and Politics in the Working-Class Suburbs of Los Angeles, 1920–1965*. Chicago: University of Chicago Press.

Nippert-Eng, Christena E. 1996. *Home and Work: Negotiating Boundaries through Everyday Life*. Chicago: University of Chicago Press.

Odih, Pamela. 2003. "Gender, Work and Organization in the Time/Space Economy of 'Just-In-Time' Labour." *Time and Society*, 12 (2/3): 293–315.

O'Mara, Margaret Pugh. 2005. "Suburbia Reconsidered: Race, Politics, and Property in the Twentieth Century." *Journal of Social History*, Fall, 39 (1): 229–44.

On Dry Land: The Desert Biome. 1991. Video recording. Northbrook Ill.: Coronet/MIT Film and Video.

Partners for Livable Communities. 2000. *The Livable City: Revitalizing Urban Communities*. New York: McGraw-Hill.

Perry, Marc. 2006. "Domestic Net Migration in the United States: 2000 to 2004." U.S. Census Bureau Report. Washington, D.C.: U.S. Department of Commerce.

REFERENCES

Pew Center. 2000. "Sprawl Now Joins Crime As Top Concern." http://www.pewcenter.org/about/pr_ST2000.html (retrieved December 18, 2005).

Phillips, Kevin. 1969. *The Emerging Republican Majority*. New Rochelle, N.Y.: Arlington House.

Phoenix Business Journal. October 8, 1999. "Serious Advice for Our Leaders." Opinion section. http://www.bizjournals.com/phoenix/stories/1999/10/11/editorial4.html (retrieved February 25, 2006).

Phoenix Chamber of Commerce. http://www.phoenixchamber.com/out_Relocate.cfm (retrieved February 5, 2002).

———. "Visitor Information." http://www.phoenixchamber.com/Visitor Information/index.asp (retrieved April 14, 2005).

Putnam, Robert D. 2000. *Bowling Alone: The Collapse and Revival of American Community*. New York: Simon & Schuster.

Quammen, David. 197. *Song of the Dodo: Island Biogeography in an Age of Extinctions*. New York: Scribner.

Rayner, Lisa. "Money with Care Built In." *Flagstaff Neighborly Notes*. http://www.flagteaparty.org/Subjects/FNN/Moneywithcarebuiltin.html (retrieved March 6, 2006).

Razen, Eran. 1998. "Policies to Control Urban Sprawl: Planning Regulations or Changes in the 'Rule of the Game.'" *Urban Studies*, February, 35 (2): 321–340.

Reisner, Mark. 1993. *Cadillac Desert: The American West and Its Disappearing Water*. New York: Penguin Books.

Rimsza, Skip. 2001. "State of the City 2001." http://phoenix.gov/CITYGOV/electidx.html (retrieved February 3, 2002).

Ritzer, George. 1993. *The McDonaldization of Society*. Newbury Park, Calif.: Pine Forge Press.

Rogers, Tim. "Majority of Homes Being Built Are Part of a Master-Planned Community." http:phoenix.about.com/cs/real/a/masterplanned.htm (retrieved December 30, 2005).

Romanyshyn, Robert. 1992. *Technology as Symptom and Dream*. New York: Routledge.

Russell, Frank. 1908/1975. *The Pima Indians*. Tucson, Ariz.: The University of Arizona Press.

Salt River Pima–Maricopa Indian Community. *General Development Plan: December, 1988*.

———. "SRPMIC Economic Development." http://www.saltriver.pima-maricopa.nsn.us/entdevco.html (retrieved May 5, 2004).

———. "Why SRPMIC." http://www.saltriver.pima-maricopa.nsn.us/whysrpmic.html (retrieved May 5, 2004).

———. "The Community." http://www.saltriver.pima-maricopa.nsn.us/seal.htm (retrieved September 19, 2004).

Saunders, Dero A. 2006. Quote under penname John P. Grier in "The Painter's Keys." http://www.painterskeys.com/auth_search.asp?name=John%20P.%20Grier (retrieved October 12, 2006).

REFERENCES

Scott, David. 1999. *Refashioning Futures: Criticism after Postcoloniality.* Princeton, N.J.: Princeton University Press.

Shaw, Anna Moore. 1968/1992. *Pima Indian Legends.* Tucson: University of Arizona Press.

Sherman, Ercell. 2002. Anthem Community Management. *Come Play with Us: Anthem Activities Guide and Information,* Fall. Anthem, Ariz.

Shiva, Vandana, ed. 1994. *Close to Home: Women Reconnect Ecology, Health and Development Worldwide.* Philadelphia: New Society Publishers.

Sides, Josh. 2004. *L.A. City Limits: African Americans in Los Angeles from the Great Depression to the Present.* Berkeley: University of California Press.

Sierra Club. 1998. "Sprawl Meets the Wild: Dishonorable Mention in Phoenix." http://www.sierraclub.org/transportation/sprawl/index.htm (retrieved November 2, 1999).

———. "Forests Main." http://www.sierraclub.org/forests/ (retrieved April 11, 2004).

Silverman, Amy. May 27, 1999. *Phoenix New Times.* "Quit Fiddling Around with Spur Cross Ranch's Owners, and Condemn the Land." http://www.phoenix newtimes.com/issues/1999–05-27/news/columns_print.html (retrieved January 29, 2006).

Sonoran Desert Conservation Plan. http://web.ask.com/redir?u=http%3a%2f%2f www.pima.gov%2fcmo%2fsdcp%2fintro.htm (retrieved April 14, 2005).

Sontag, Deborah. 2003. "The Power of the Fourth." *New York Times Magazine,* March 9, Section 6: 38–45, 54, 65, 77, 80.

Southern Arizona Adventures. 2006. http://www.arizonatour.com/ (retrieved January 25, 2006).

Steen, Harold K. 1976. *The U.S. Forest Service: A History.* Seattle: University of Washington Press.

Stone, Christopher D. 1972/1988. *Should Trees Have Standing: Toward Legal Rights for Natural Objects.* Palo Alto, Calif.: Tiogo.

Stuart, Don. 2003. "Protecting the Land that Sustains Us." American Farmland Trust. http://www.farmland.org/research/publications_download.htm (retrieved December 17, 2005).

Suzuki, David, and Amanda McConnell. 1999. *The Sacred Balance: Rediscovering Our Place in Nature.* Seattle: Mountaineers.

Swaback, Vernon D. 1997. *Designing the Future.* Phoenix: Herberger Center for Design.

Swan, James A., and Roberta Swan. 2000. *Bound to the Earth.* Lincoln, Nebr.: iUniverse.com.

Thoreau, Henry David. 1854/1973. *Walden.* Princeton, N.J.: Princeton University Press.

Town of Cave Creek General Plan 1993. Cave Creek: Ariz.

Tropiano, Dolores. 2002. "Eco-Homes Part of the Landscape." *Arizona Republic,* August 13: B4.

REFERENCES

Tuan, Yi Fu. 1993. *Passing Strange and Wonderful: Aesthetics, Nature, and Culture.* Washington, D.C.: Island Press.

Turner, Victor. 1974. *Dramas, Fields and Metaphors: Symbolic Action in Human Society.* Ithaca, N.Y.: Cornell University Press.

United Nations. 1992. *Adoption of Agreements on Environment and Development: Agenda 21.* United Nations Conference on Environment and Development, Rio de Janeiro, 3–14, June, 1992. A/CONF.151/4 (Part1), Chapter 12, 12.2.

Updike, John. 1979. *Problems and Other Stories.* New York: Knopf.

U.S. Census Bureau. Census 2000. PHC-T-2. Ranking Tables for Incorporated Places of 100,000 or More: 1990 to 2000. Table 2 Incorporated Places of 100,000 or More, Ranked by Population: 2000.

———. Census 2000. PHC-T-3. Ranking Tables for Metropolitan Areas 1990 and 2000. Table 3 Metropolitan Areas Ranked by Population: 2000.

———. Census 2000. Table 4 Metropolitan Areas Ranked by Numeric Population Change 1990 to 2000.

———. 2006. Fact Finder, 2006 Population Estimate for Phoenix, Arizona. http://factfinder.census.gov. (retrieved January 12, 2008).

U.S. Bureau News. 2003. "Nevada, Arizona Major Destinations of Late '90s Exodus from California, Census Bureau Reports." http://www.census.gov/Press-Release/www/2003/cb03cn62.htm/ (retrieved January 12, 2008).

———. 2005. "Largest Census-to-Census Population Increase in U.S. History As Every State Gains, Census Bureau Reports." http://www.census.gov/Press-Release/www/releases/archives/census_2000/000718.html (retrieved April 5, 2005).

Voltaire. 1759/1959. *Candide.* New York: Bantam Books.

Voto, Bernard De. "Sage's Sayings." http://members.aol.com/thomask2/wildwest-show/wws1a.html (retrieved January 24, 2006).

Warner, Kee, and Harvey Molotch. 2001. *Building Rules: How Local Controls Shape Community Environments and Economies.* Boulder, Colo.: Westview Press.

Warren, Karen. 2004. "The Philosophical Foundation of a New Land Ethic." In *The Land Ethic Toolbox: Using Ethics, Emotion and Spiritual Values to Advance American Land Conservation*, edited by Robert T. Perschel, 12–16. Washington, D.C.: The Wilderness Society

Washington, George. 1789. First Inaugural Address. Founder's Library. http://www.founding.com/library/lbody.cfm?id=195&parent=60 (retrieved January 17, 2006).

Weatherby, James B., and Stephanie L. Witt. 1994. *The Urban West: Managing Growth and Decline.* Westport, Conn.: Praeger.

Weber, Max. 1914/1978. *Economy and Society: An Outline of Interpretive Sociology.* Berkeley: University of California Press.

Wilber, Ken. 1996. *A Brief History of Everything.* Boston: Shambhala.

Wilkinson, Charles F. 1999. *Fire on the Plateau: Conflict and Endurance in the American Southwest.* Washington, D.C.: Island Press.

REFERENCES

Wilson, William H. 1983. "Moles and Skylarks." In *Introduction to Planning History in the United States*, edited by Donald A. Krueckeberg, 88–121. New Brunswick, N.J.: Center for Urban Policy Research.

Weaver, Jace. 1997. *Defending Mother Earth: Native American Perspectives on Environmental Justice*. New York: Maryknoll.

W. P. Carey School of Business. 2001. Press Release. https://129.219.60.118/top/pressrelease_display.cfm?num=328 (retrieved January 12, 2008).

Zerubavel, Eviatar. 1981. *Hidden Rhythms: Schedules and Calendars in Social Life*. Chicago: University of Chicago Press.

———. 1985. *The Seven Day Circle: The History and Meaning of the Week*. New York: Free Press.

———. 1991. *The Fine Line: Making Distinctions in Everyday Life*. New York: Free Press

———. 1997. Social Mindscapes: An Invitation to Cognitive Sociology. Cambridge, Mass.: Harvard University Press.

———. 2003. *Time Maps: Collective Memory and the Social Shape of the Past*. Chicago: University of Chicago Press.

INDEX

141

Photovoltaics, 58, 110
Pima: creation story, 25, 27–30;
history of, 23; legends, 25, 28,
108; reburial ceremonies, 30;
worldview, 31. *See also* Hoo-
hoogam; Salt River
Pima-Maricopa Indian
Community
Pima Freeway (Loop 101), 24, 28,
30, 73; relocation, 73–74
Pima "Man in the Maze symbol," 28
Planning industry, 34–36, 79; city
planners, 34–36, 74, 75, 78, 88,
92, 98, 119; regional planning,
76, 116
Plato, 61
Pollution Prevention Act (PPA), 98
Population growth, 89
Poverty, 73
Power Ranch, 65–66
Preservation, 6, 7, 31, 49, 72, 75,
76, 92, 94, 99, 102–104, 108–
109, 111–12, 123n3. *See also*
Land Ethic
Private property, 40, 75, 95, 97, 112
Property rights, 6, 8, 55, 69, 82, 89,
94–112
Pueblos, 93
Putnam, Robert, 76, 126n5

Quammen, David, 76

Rational society, 18, 21–38, 39, 40,
48, 53, 55–56, 59, 60, 61, 62,
104. *See also* Modernity; Science
Real estate, 34, 35, 36, 50
Real Simple (magazine), 79
Recreation, 51, 52, 65, 66, 84. *See
also* Amenities
Regan, Ronald, 98
Renewable energy. *See* Electricity
Reservations. *See* Native American
communities
Resources. *See* Utilitarianism

Responsible development, 8, 36, 47,
57–61, 85, 93, 122
Rights and responsibilities, 102–
104, 111
Rights of nature, 103–104
Rimsza, Skip (Phoenix Mayor), 4
Riparian areas, 6, 96, 123n1
Rural. *See under* Land
Russell, Frank, 27

Saguaro cactus, 5, 6, 9, 11, 45, 49,
115
Salt River, 13, 21, 23, 24, 42, 46, 92
Salt River Pima–Maricopa Indian
Community, 11, 13, 19, 21, 23–
24, 27–33, 36, 37, 56, 64, 72–74,
85, 92, 107–108, 111, 124n3;
elders in, 42–47, 60, 108, 113;
population of, 24; research in,
119–22. *See also* Pima
Salt River Project, 42–43
A Sand County Almanac (Leopold),
101–102
San Francisco Peaks, 27
Scraping. *See* Blading
Science, 31, 33–36; Scientific
Revolution, 33–34, 61. *See also*
Rational society
Scottsdale, Ariz., 4, 13, 47, 80, 84,
104
Segregation, 59
Simple living, 79, 81
Situated knowledge, 14
Smart Growth, 8
Social activism, 6, 108, 115–16. *See
also* Community building
Social cement (Marcuse), 90
Social change, 27, 35–36, 79, 115–
16
Social research, 14–20, 119–22
Solar panels. *See* Photovoltaics
SONG Neighborhood (Ithaca,
N.Y.), 106
Sonora, Mexico, 9

INDEX